LEGAL GUIDE TO
SOCIAL
MEDIA

NOV 22 2013

LEGAL GUIDE TO
SOCIAL
MEDIA

rights and risks for
businesses and entrepreneurs

Kimberly A. Houser

ALLWORTH PRESS
NEW YORK

Allworth Press books may be purchased in bulk at special discounts for sales promotion, corporate gifts, fund-raising, or educational purposes. Special editions can also be created to specifications. For details, contact the Special Sales Department, Allworth Press, 307 West 36th Street, 11th Floor, New York, NY 10018 or info@skyhorsepublishing.com.

17 16 15 14 13 5 4 3 2 1

Published by Allworth Press, an imprint of Skyhorse Publishing, Inc.
307 West 36th Street, 11th Floor, New York, NY 10018.

Allworth Press® is a registered trademark of Skyhorse Publishing, Inc.®, a Delaware corporation.

www.allworth.com

Cover and interior design by Mary Belibasakis
Page composition/typography by Integra Software Services, Pvt., Ltd., Pondicherry, India

Library of Congress Cataloging-in-Publication Data is available on file

ISBN: 978-1-62153-267-5

Printed in the United States of America

For my daughter, Anastasia Nicole

CONTENTS

ACKNOWLEDGEMENTS

I would like to thank everyone at Allworth Press for being so organized and walking me through the entire process, especially Tad Crawford, Delia Casa, and Thornwell May.

I send a heartfelt thanks to the businesswomen who helped me come up with topics for this legal guide: Sandra Esse DiBona, Anney Smith, Vicky Rudy, and Amy Schubert. I also want to express appreciation to my "boss," Chris Harman, for his enthusiasm about this book and to my high school drama teacher, Joe Gerace, who encouraged me to write this book while he was writing his.

I am also grateful to my two best friends Ken Jones and Laurie Swanson Oberhelman whom I have known since high school. Both had unflappable faith that this book would be published and both cheered me on every step of the way. Ken never let me doubt myself and Laurie held me accountable on a daily basis during the last month of the project—no small feat.

I would also like to thank my friends, my current and former students, and all of my clients for trusting me with their questions and encouraging me in my writing.

INTRODUCTION

If You Are in Social Media Marketing and Have Posted Content Online or Set Up a Website Without Consulting an Attorney, Help Is on the Way!

Facebook, Twitter, YouTube—we all use them. We all view them. But do we really know whether what we post is legal? Do we really think through each word we type prior to hitting send? Do people really take those Facebook posts seriously? Donald Trump did. In December 2012, an arbitrator ordered Sheena Monnin, a contestant in the Miss USA pageant, to pay the Miss Universe Organization (owned by Donald Trump) $5 million for defamatory statements she posted on Facebook.[1] This is one of several high-profile cases involving allegedly defamatory statements on Facebook. Tweets have also resulted in legal troubles for those who post them. The NBA fined Dallas Mavericks owner Mark Cuban $50,000 for tweeting about the officiating after a Mavericks game on January 5, 2013.[2] This of course is nothing compared to the $500,000 fine against Micky Arison for a tweet he made during the 2011 NBA lockout.[3]

In the past few years we have seen a dramatic increase in lawsuits being filed and fines assessed against people posting comments and videos on the Internet. This increase in lawsuits and fines corresponds with the recent explosion of the use of social media. In 2012, Facebook reported over 1 billion active users up from 150 million users in 2009.

Social media marketing is the use of interactive websites to promote services and products. Unlike traditional one-way advertisements, social media sites permit consumers the ability to converse directly with the advertisers as well as endorse or denounce products and services on their own. HubSpot reported that in 2010 advertisers spent almost $1.7 billion on social media marketing.[4] Marketing Profs estimates that expenditures will exceed $4.6 billion by 2016.[5]

Social media marketing includes a wide variety of activities; however, it has a singular purpose: to generate business through Internet sites. According to Mashable, "social media marketing programs usually center on efforts to create content that attracts attention and encourages readers to share it with their social networks. A corporate message spreads from user to user and presumably resonates because it appears to come from a trusted, third-party source, as opposed to the brand or company itself. Hence, this form of marketing is driven by word-of-mouth, meaning it results in earned media rather than paid media."[6] This includes setting up websites; setting up social media profiles; creating content; monitoring social media; linking to other websites; blogging; posting comments on websites, blogs, and social media sites; posting videos and podcasts on websites, blogs, or social media sites; and much more.

The legal issues are varied and the implications enormous, both for the companies and advertisers trying to "control" conversations about their products and services, and for the consumer who takes it upon himself or herself to generate content about a product or service. Social media marketing differs from traditional marketing in that the marketing efforts are no longer outbound. They include inbound messaging and viral messaging. The message can take on a life of its own, sometimes leading to a "telephone game" result. Companies and advertisers attempting to influence consumers through the Internet have to deal with a host of unpredictable results. If there is one thing the law likes, it is predictability. The advantage of the social media marketers is their narrow focus and ability to monitor messages and consumers in a way that most large businesses cannot. The disadvantage is that laws regarding traditional forms of advertising are being applied to new technologies in ways that cannot be anticipated.

Despite the easy entry into this field, many users of social media are not aware of the enormous legal risks involved in their online activities. These risks include violating state and federal advertising laws, copyright laws, privacy laws, securities laws, trademark laws, and tort laws such as defamation. Many people engaged in social media marketing are regularly posting on websites belonging to others without understanding how such a website's terms of use could affect them. In addition to liability for their own posts, there is also the potential to become liable for third-party content posted to their own sites. The jurisdictional issues alone are mind-boggling. A Louisiana resident posting comments on a website about a Florida resident could inadvertently expose herself to a lawsuit in Florida based on that state's defamation laws.

How can social media marketers avoid being sued or fined for posts they didn't even know were violations of the law? The easy answer is by becoming informed. Unfortunately, there are not many places to look for this type of information. There is a great deal of false information posted on the Internet by non-attorneys regarding the legalities of social media marketing efforts. The legal websites and blogs out there simply describe recent lawsuits, which may be frightening but are not particularly helpful. The government websites only talk about the laws in their jurisdiction. None give practical advice on avoiding violations, and many contain inaccurate or outdated information. The most common types of risks, however, can be avoided by taking simple steps before, during, and after engaging in online activities.

Because legal books can be so overwhelming for the average person, I have crafted the *Legal Guide to Social Media* in a simple question-and-answer format. I now receive as many questions from clients about posting content online and making sure their websites are "legal" as I do about how to form a corporation or LLC. This wasn't the case just a few years ago.

Many of my clients who started with a website or blog now actively participate in social media sites. Some of my clients have businesses that operate 100 percent online, and others make their money using social media to promote their business and the businesses of others. When I look at their activities, I am often surprised by what I find there. I found some of my clients copying terms of use and privacy policies from other websites. They told me that they figured that since they took it from a big company's website, a team of lawyers probably prepared it. Besides the obvious copyright infringement issues, I have pointed out that this simple act could result in millions of dollars in damages. In the case of *CollegeNet v. XAP*, D. Ore. No. 03-CV-1229 (2008), XAP was found to have engaged in deceptive trade practices when the company sold its users' personal information to financial institutions contrary to its privacy policy. Even though its privacy policy specifically indicated that personal data would not be shared with third parties without the users' express consent, XAP violated its own policy by sharing the data without the express consent of its users. CollegeNet sued for damages (as this conduct affected its business) and was awarded $5.4 million. The lesson here is that when you copy someone else's privacy policy and it does not match what you actually do, you could be found liable for damages. What XAP did was deceptive because the company led its users to believe the information they provided while using the site would be kept private. If you copy someone's privacy policy or draft one on your own that indicates that you do not share information when you actually do, you could be held liable under a number of legal theories. The law is changing rapidly to take into account online activities. It is difficult enough for the Internet lawyer to keep up; it is even more difficult for the non-lawyer.

Designed for the non-lawyer, this guide addresses the legal issues involved in social media marketing but will also be helpful to anyone with an online presence. There are ten chapters, each covering a different legal risk area. The topics covered are: defamation; infringement issues; laws concerning advertising, privacy, and employment; intellectual property rights; hosting websites and blogs; and legal considerations for e-business startups.

1 DEFAMATION AND OTHER
TORT RISKS IN POSTING CONTENT

In the Florida Internet defamation case, *Scheff v. Bock*, the court awarded $11.4 million to Scheff as a result of her claim of Internet defamation. In this case, Bock, a woman unhappy with the services provided by Scheff, began making negative posts on a number of websites and forums regarding Scheff's business, which the court found to be defamatory.

While it is true that you have a right of free speech, that right is limited. Although "truth" is a complete defense to defamation, the problem occurs when you cannot prove the truth or have to defend yourself against a lawsuit outside of your own jurisdiction. In this case, the defendant, who lived in Louisiana, was unable to afford to defend herself in Florida, resulting in this large judgment against her. This chapter will discuss the three types of activities most likely to result in a lawsuit.

Torts are "civil wrongs," which means the law provides a remedy in civil court for harm caused to tort victims by others. Torts can be either intentional or negligent. Defamation would be an example of an intentional tort. Negligence occurs when someone fails to use due care, which results in someone else being injured. This chapter will discuss some of the misconceptions that people have about liability for their online activities (for example, there is no right to anonymity on the Internet—contrary to popular belief). It explains how even though a blog or Facebook post may seem like a casual conversation among friends, it is actually a permanent publication that can never be completely retracted from cyberspace. It explains what types of posts constitute a breach of privacy, breach of right of publicity, and defamation, as well as the steps the readers can take to protect themselves from these types of claims.

1.1 WHAT IS DEFAMATION?

Defamation occurs when all of the following elements converge:
1. A statement is made
2. The statement is to a third party
3. The statement is about another person
4. The statement is false, and
5. The statement is likely to harm the person's reputation.

The laws of the states vary in this definition and what is required in terms of proof, but these are the most common elements. Let's take the elements one by one.

1. The statement must be of an alleged fact, or it must be a statement of opinion that is presented as a fact. There is an additional element of malice that must be proven when the statement is about a public figure. The statement can be either written or oral. Libel is a defamatory statement put into fixed form, whereas slander is a spoken defamatory statement. Posts and videos placed on the Internet are technically libel since they are put into fixed form.

2. The statement must be made to a third party, which is known as publication. In other words, if you tell someone to his face that he is a crook, there is no defamation because there is no publication. Although widespread communication is not required, even if "no one" reads your post, there is publication. In addition, if you are repeating something that you hear that is defamatory, you have committed defamation yourself—this is true even if you indicate where you heard it. Thus, retweeting can subject you to a defamation claim.

3. The statement has to be about a particular person or entity. A corporation can be defamed if a false statement affects the business's integrity, credit, or solvency. Product disparagement is very similar to corporate defamation except it involves false statements about a company's products or services and is sometimes alleged hand in hand with corporate defamation. If you identify a person by his or her first and last name, it is easy to prove that you named a particular person. You are still liable if you label someone as "my boss" or "my last boyfriend," because they are still identifiable. The person must also be alive to be defamed.

4. The statement must be false. Although truth is a defense to defamation, it is difficult to prove without written documentation. Of course,

even if you have the proof, it can cost quite a bit of money to defend yourself in court. For example, if you state on your blog that "John Smith stole office supplies from his place of employment," and you saw him do this, you may feel confident that this statement is completely and undeniably true. However, when John gets on the stand and says he did not steal anything, you have a proof problem. It is his word against your word. If the judge or jury believes him and not you, you will be held liable. However, even if you did have a videotape and written confession of the theft, if he sues you, you still have to defend yourself in court, which can be a costly proposition.

5. The statement must be likely to harm someone's reputation. Stating someone is a crook will most likely cause damage to that person. It is very easy to imagine that it will hurt his employment prospects at the very least. There are several types of statements that are considered libel per se: allegations of criminal conduct, contagious diseases, impotence, lack of virginity, or lack of qualification in his profession. Libel per se permits private individuals and public figures to bring a claim without having to prove damages.

I cannot stress enough how the laws in different states can result in different results. Look at the different results in California and Oregon to get a feeling for why this matters. In *O'Grady v. Superior Court*,[7] the California Court of Appeals held that online reporters could keep their sources confidential under the journalist protection required by the First Amendment. Apple had sued several unnamed reporters who posted information about some new Apple products prior to their being available to the public. In Oregon, a federal judge determined that an online reporter was not a journalist, and the failure to recognize her blog as a news report (which would have required the plaintiff to meet a higher standard of proof) resulted in a $2.5 million defamation judgment against her.[8]

If the defamatory statement does not fall within the category of libel per se, the person defamed will usually have to provide some proof of damages.[9] The types of damages awarded can include compensation for the harm to the plaintiff's reputation, and punitive damages if the statement is outrageous. In some defamation suits the plaintiff merely wants the offending statement removed. Because state law varies on what is recoverable and what proof is required, it is not possible to provide a rule of thumb. Just know that regarding the potential for being held liable, you will always have to pay an attorney to defend you whether you win or lose.

1.2 HOW DO I AVOID A LAWSUIT FOR DEFAMATION?

As discussed, defamation occurs when false information is published about a person that is likely to injure the person's reputation. Defamation can result from an oral statement (slander) or a written statement (libel). Libel includes any statement put into fixed form by being written, broadcast, or published electronically. Since online communications are deemed to be libel, they are more difficult to defend and can result in higher damages.

There is the additional element of malice when someone is writing about a public figure.[10] The definition of a public figure has been expanded over time. It includes not only public officials and celebrities but also those who become inserted into the public eye. It is believed that those who actively seek public attention should expect to have news reports made about their activities to a greater extent than a private individual. Thus, malice means knowledge of falsity or a reckless disregard for the truth.

There are a number of defenses to defamation. These include truth, opinion, fair report, consent, and retraction. I will discuss each of these individually.

Truth: It is often said that truth is a complete defense to defamation. This is true, but you have to look at it from a proof perspective. If you feel strongly that your statement is true, you need to ask yourself what proof you have. Remember, just because you believe something to be true doesn't mean the jury will side with you if the person suing you makes a convincing story that what you said was false.

Opinion: One of the elements of defamation is that the statement has to be of a verifiable fact. Indicating that someone is an asshole in a blog post is not defamation. You cannot "verify" that someone is an asshole. It is your opinion. If you call someone a crook, however, the connotation is that this person tends to steal things. This is verifiable and thus defamation. The standard that the courts use is whether or not a reasonable person would believe you are describing actual facts (not whether you call the statement an opinion).[11]

Fair report: The fair reports defense protects fair and true reports of judicial, legislative, or other official proceedings. In California this defense has been applied to online postings made on an online message board.[12] A "fair and true" report must reflect the gist of the proceedings. It does not have to be a verbatim account. It must also indicate the source and not be misleading.[13]

Consent: As with any intentional tort, "the consent of another to the publication of defamatory matter concerning him is a complete defense to his action for defamation."[14] What this means is that if you were given permission by the parties whom you are writing about to make the statement, they cannot later claim defamation. It is always important to document in writing any consent.

Retraction: Although not technically a defense, since you can still be sued for defamation even after a retraction, certain states have retraction statutes, which will reduce your liability for defamation. A great guide to each state's retraction laws can be found on the Citizen's Media Law website at www.citmedialaw.org/legal-guide/state-law-retractions. Many times, the harmed party merely wants the offending material removed and if you comply, will not sue you.

There is not, however, a First Amendment right of free speech defense to defamation. A former student at the University of Michigan recently obtained a $4.5 million judgment against a former assistant attorney general who defamed the student online through a blog he created for that purpose.[15] The only defense presented by the defendant was that he had a First Amendment right to air his opinions about the plaintiff. The court indicated that this right did not extend to making false statements about the plaintiff and that nothing posted by the defendant was an actual opinion.

There are a number of preventative strategies that you can utilize in order to avoid a lawsuit for defamation. These have traditionally been used by reporters but are also great advice for anyone who posts online. 1. Verify the information prior to posting. If you investigate the information, this will help with your defense. Obviously, if you can find no confirmation of what you wish to post, your best bet is to not post it. 2. Do not retweet indiscriminately. This is a huge issue today because of the ease with which you can forward defamatory information. Unless you either verify the information contained in the original tweet or are very sure about the reliability of the source, do not retweet. 3. If you do check out the information or receive consent, maintain the written records (or at the very least note in your datebook what you found out in your investigation). 4. Identify your source. If you are posting information that may be harmful to someone, make sure you indicate where you found this information. While this may not be a complete defense, it will mitigate your liability somewhat. 5. Watch your descriptions of identifiable people. Again, indicating that someone is a crook could lead to liability, whereas calling someone an asshole will not. Remember, opinions and nonverifiable statements are generally not defamatory. 6. Review the list of libel per se topics, and stay away from them![16]

1.3 DON'T I HAVE THE RIGHT TO ANONYMITY ON THE INTERNET?

The Supreme Court has said that citizens do have the right to anonymous free speech in the United States. In *McIntyre v. Ohio Elections Commission*,[17] the Ohio law requiring the names of the authors of political pamphlets to be disclosed was declared unconstitutional, and the courts have been fairly consistent in striking down any statutes disallowing anonymous free speech. The First Amendment does not, however, provide a right of anonymity with respect to tortious or criminal speech. What this means with respect to anonymous posts on the Internet is that the identity of the poster can be discovered under certain circumstances. Courts have permitted what are known as "Jane or John Doe subpoenas" to be issued, which requires the Internet service provider to identify the subscriber to a particular IP address involved in allegedly tortious or criminal conduct. This is contrary to the widely distributed and repeated belief that you have the right to remain anonymous on the Internet.

In *Polito v. AOL Time Warner*,[18] the court used a balancing test to determine whether to require the identity of an online poster to be revealed. The right of privacy and free speech was compared with the victim's right to obtain the identity of the online poster who harmed her in order to hold him accountable. The court ultimately issued the subpoena requiring the Internet server provider to disclose the offender's identity.

In the case of *Stone v. Paddock Publications*,[19] an Illinois court issued a subpoena to obtain the identity of an anonymous poster but then indicated that the poster would be kept anonymous until the plaintiff was able to show that he had been harmed. The plaintiff had asked the court to issue a subpoena to identify the defendant who made allegedly defamatory posts regarding the plaintiff under an assumed name. During arguments, the anonymous poster (hipcheck16) argued through his attorney that his identity should be protected as being engaged in anonymous political speech under either the Illinois anti-SLAPP statute or the First Amendment.

The Illinois court, in citing the case of two Yale law students who were defamed on a website and were able to obtain the identity of the posters—*Doe I v. Individuals*, 561 F. Supp. 249 (D Conn. 2008)—ruled that the First Amendment does not protect posters' identities from being discovered when they have engaged in speech which is not protected. The judge in *Stone* adopted the six-part test in *Doe*: 1. The defendant must be given notice of the subpoena and an opportunity to object. 2. The plaintiff must identify the offending post. 3. The plaintiff must have no other way to discover the identity of the defendant. 4. The subpoenaed information must be necessary to the case. 5. The poster must not have a right to anonymity. 6. The plaintiff must make an adequate showing that the case has merit.

The Illinois court found that although the first five elements had been met, it could not go so far as to say that the plaintiff had made an adequate showing that the case had merit, because the case against the poster had not yet been filled. The court took the unusual route of obtaining hipcheck16's identity but ordering that it not be revealed except to the plaintiff, her attorney, and the process server until such time as the trial court could rule on the sixth element.

There have been an increasing number of lawsuits being brought against anonymous posters of comments on the Internet. Although the courts throughout the states have varied widely in their reasoning for issuing or denying subpoenas, most judges try to balance the rights of the poster with the right of the plaintiff to bring an action. While some critics of these types of rulings have indicated that the plaintiff should not have to prove her case prior to discovering the identity of the defendant, others have argued that it is necessary to protect the right of free speech. Regardless, the First Amendment does not give anyone the right to defame another.[20]

Electronic communications are subject to the same laws and regulations as any other communications. As discussed in question 1.1, if you make a damaging false statement about a person or entity, you could be subject to a claim for defamation or corporate defamation (or product disparagement). If you reveal personal and private information (sexual, medical, and financial) about a person without his or her consent, you could be subject to a claim for invasion of privacy. If you use someone's likeness or name without his or her consent, you could be subject to a claim for misappropriation. As you can see, you want to verify the information that you post and make sure that it is true and published with consent when appropriate.

Because it is very easy to forget that you are not just venting to a friend, unchecked posting can lead to trouble. I often caution my clients to cool off before responding to an issue that upsets them. While a blog is a wonderful vehicle for getting your opinions out there, you must always remember that it is a permanent record of your statement. Even if you delete it, it still exists in cyberspace.

You should also be aware of the following torts that can arise in situations involving websites and blogs: defamation, trade libel (or product disparagement), invasion of privacy, and misappropriation. Defamation occurs when you make a false or misleading statement about a person or entity in front of others and thus cause harm to the person or entity defamed. Clearly a post on a website or blog would be considered "published." Trade libel or product disparagement occurs when you make a false or misleading statement about someone else's products or services. Invasion of privacy occurs when you use someone's name, image, or other information under circumstances that would cause them embarrassment. Because each state's laws are different, it is hard to summarize, but at a minimum you would want to avoid disclosing facts about people that a reasonable person would consider private (e.g., sexual preferences), using someone's name or photo for your own commercial purposes (e.g., a photo-shopped image of a celebrity holding your product), disclosing embarrassing private facts about someone in a public forum (e.g., posting photos taken at 2 AM at a party), and intruding on someone's privacy in a highly offensive manner (e.g., cell phone photos taken in a locker room). Your best bet is to obtain a release form for any pictures you post and any names you use.

If there is any potential for a tort or criminal claim, do not rely on the protection of the Internet to remain anonymous. Your identity can be discovered.

1.4 DOESN'T THE COMMUNICATIONS DECENCY ACT PROTECT ME?

It does not protect you from posts made by you: It only protects you from posts made by others on your website under certain circumstances. The Communications Decency Act (CDA)[21] does not provide immunity for bloggers as some have reported. It only provides protection, under certain circumstance, for material and information posted by *someone else* on your blog or website. If you have a blog or website which permits users to post information there, you will have some protection through the CDA. The act does provide that offending statements made by others on your blog or website will not subject you to liability. This protection does not extend to your own posts (or those made under your direction or by employees). However, under certain circumstances you could be subject to what is called secondary liability for items posted by others on your website (i.e., if you knew or should have known of the nature of the material). Your best bet is to monitor postings and remove potentially damaging ones. This is one of the reasons to include a terms of use on your blog or website.[22]

What liability seems to depend on is whether you actually monitor the comments to your blog. If you do have an approval process (i.e., comments do not appear unless you "approve" them), and a defamatory comment slips through, you are more likely to be subject to liability than if you set up your website to approve all comments. Your best option, however, is to truly monitor your site.

Rather than relying on the Communications Decency Act to protect you from liability, you should make sure your terms of use indicate that offending material (including defamatory statements) may not be posted and that you have the right to edit and delete all posts at any time. This way, you can remove posts or edit out questionable portions of posts.

Please note that the CDA does not apply to intellectual property issues; thus if someone posts something that infringes on someone else's trademark or copyright, you could be liable. Under the theory of contributory infringement, you can be held liable for someone else's posts. Contributory infringement occurs where someone knowingly assists in infringing activity. For example, if your friend makes a copy of a DVD and you know these copies are an infringement but you help create his website to sell them, you would be liable under the theory of contributory infringement. Vicarious liability (which is liability for another's actions) for infringement can occur without your knowledge when you either are responsible for supervising the activity or had a financial interest in the outcome. For example, if you have an employee who makes blog posts for you occasionally and then posts something that he copied from another site, you could be vicariously liable for his action.

1.5 DON'T ANTI-SLAPP LAWS PROTECT ME?

If you do get sued for defamation, there are some defenses you can assert, including truth. However, you will need to get an attorney. If you believe that the First Amendment protects the statement you made, your attorney can check if your state has an anti-SLAPP law.[23] A SLAPP (strategic lawsuit against public participation) is a lawsuit that is intended to silence critics by burdening them with the cost of defending a legal action against them. Instead of presenting a valid legal argument, the plaintiff merely hopes that his or her threat will result in the blogger removing the post. California's anti-SLAPP law specifically applies to any writing made in connection with an issue under consideration by the legislative, executive, or judicial branch. You would, however, be entitled to your attorney fees if you won. Each state's law is different.

The idea behind the anti-SLAPP laws is to make it more difficult for those bringing lawsuits regarding protected speech based on a dislike of what is being said and hoping the threat will force the material to be removed. In the case of *Barrett v. Rosenthal*,[24] Rosenthal was sued for an allegedly defamatory letter that was posted on her website about the plaintiffs. The California Supreme Court ruled that all but one count of the lawsuit had to be dismissed under Section 230 of the Communications Decency Act, which protected Rosenthal from civil liability for the republication of the words of others. The court also granted Rosenthal's motion under California's anti-SLAPP statute,[25] which resulted in an award of $434,000 in attorney fees (which was later reduced).

Another option is to obtain a media liability insurance policy to cover online libel claims. Because of the potential for large judgments, the cost of defending a defamation suit, and the expense of maintaining insurance to cover these types of claims, your best course of action is to monitor your posts so that you do not defame anyone.

1.6 CAN I BE SUED FOR DEFAMATORY ITEMS POSTED ON MY BLOG OR WEBSITE BY OTHERS?

The simple answer is yes, it is possible. If you have an interactive component on your website which allows others to post comments, there is a potential for a lawsuit by someone harmed by what is posted on your site even if you did not post it. If, for example, someone posts a defamatory comment about another person, you could also be liable in some states (in addition to the person who made the post) for defamation.

In general, one who repeats a defamatory statement is just as liable as the original speaker.[26] But if you are considered an Internet service provider under Section 230(c) of the Communications Decency Act of 1996 ("CDA"),[27] you may have immunity. If you are considered an Internet content provider, you might not. Section 230(c)(1) of the CDA states, "No cause of action may be brought and no liability may be imposed under any State or local law that is inconsistent with this section." Section 230(c)(2) provides: "No provider or user of an interactive computer service shall be held liable on account of—(A) any action voluntarily taken in good faith to restrict access to or availability of material that the provider or user considers to be obscene, lewd, lascivious, filthy, excessively violent, harassing, or otherwise objectionable, whether or not such material is constitutionally protected; or (B) any action taken to enable or make available to information content providers or others the technical means to restrict access to material described in paragraph (1)." This is a developing area of law, and the answer does vary by jurisdiction. In addition, federal courts have not been consistent in their interpretation of the CDA. Some have held that it provides complete immunity to a website owner, and others have carved out exceptions.

The distinction between an Internet service provider and an Internet content provider is very important. In *Fair Housing v. Roommates.com*,[28] the court held that the website Roommates.com was not immune from liability under Section 230 of the CDA, because it was not merely permitting users to post on the site but was also partly responsible for contributing the offending material in the way the website was structured. There have been several other cases that have made the distinction between an Internet service provider and an Internet content provider.[29]

You will have some protection from the Communications Decency Act 47 U.S.C. Section 230, which was explained in section 1.4 of this book. If you do not monitor the posts made by others, you may be able to rely on Section 230 of the CDA, which states that "No provider or user of an interactive computer service shall be treated as the publisher or speaker of any information provided by another information content provider." The next question explains the procedure you must follow under this statute to gain protection.

1.7 WHAT IS BREACH OF RIGHT TO PRIVACY?

Privacy concerns vary widely among individuals. Some people are naturally shy, whereas others hog the spotlight any chance they get. Privacy rights vary from state to state. There are a number of different ways in which a person's right to privacy can be breached. A claim of public exposure of private facts occurs when private facts that a typical person would want kept private are exposed. A claim of invasion of privacy occurs when someone enters into a space that you would expect to be private. A claim of false light can occur when an individual is falsely portrayed in an offensive manner, such as putting someone's name on or next to a list of registered sex offenders. Private individuals have the right to control what information is revealed about them to the public. Different rules apply when what an individual does is newsworthy or is a public figure. Public figures have a lesser expectation of privacy.

1.8 HOW DO I AVOID A LAWSUIT FOR BREACH OF RIGHT OF PRIVACY?

As discussed in question 1.7, breach of privacy is a general term used to describe a number of different causes of action relating to one's privacy. Because the laws in different jurisdictions vary and the descriptions and elements of these claims differ from state to state, the following explanations are more encompassing than they may be in a particular state.

The first cause of action is known as public disclosure of private facts. Private information includes personal information such as sexual orientation or medical conditions. It is the information that a reasonable person would expect to be kept private. When you post private information about someone on your blog, you are making it public, which could be a violation of that person's right to privacy. Private information can be made public only when the public has a legitimate interest in knowing such information. Whether there is a legitimate reason depends on a number of factors, including the person you are writing about and the nature of the information.

For example, if your neighbor found a new job, an ordinary person would probably not consider that to be private information. On the other hand, a story about your married neighbor's new girlfriend would probably be deemed private. Whether the public would have a legitimate interest in such a story is another issue. We have seen many a politician be exposed through the media. The defense to public disclosure of private facts is consent. In other words if you are told of the private information by the person who it is about in a way which would indicate that they approve of its publication, this would be considered consent. In addition, if you post information that is available in public records, regardless of how embarrassing, this would also be a defense. Another possible defense is newsworthiness. When information that is true but private is posted, the courts will judge the legality of the post by balancing such factors as the public's right to know, the social value of the disclosure, and the status of the individual (celebrity or non-celebrity). This is not the best defense, because of the flexible nature of the court's determination.

Celebrities or public figures have a lower expectation of privacy because courts have found that they have put themselves in the public eye. Thus, many times you can post private information about a celebrity that you could not about a private individual.

The second right to privacy theory is invasion of privacy (or intrusion on privacy). Generally, in situations in which a person has a reasonable expectation of privacy, such as in one's home, it would be considered an invasion to take a photograph of such a person through a window. It would not be a breach to photograph someone in a public place under most circumstances, as long as the photo does not defame or otherwise show the person in a false light. It can also happen when someone actually intrudes a person's private domain if that would be considered offensive to the average person. Even in a public place, if someone photographed you with a hidden camera while you were bending over or with a camera positioned to look up your skirt, this would be an invasion of privacy. The gist of this claim is that the way in which the information was gathered is inappropriate. Many times a claim for criminal or civil trespass can also be alleged. The best way to avoid this type of claim is to obtain written consent to the recording of conversations or taking of photographs or video. In some states this failure to obtain written consent can result in criminal charges.

The third cause of action is false light. This type of claim occurs when the following elements are present: The information is published widely (i.e., not to just a single person, as in defamation); it identifies the plaintiff specifically; it places the plaintiff in a "false light" that would be highly offensive to a reasonable person; and the defendant was responsible for publishing the information.[30]

This happens often with photographs or names being placed next to text that appears to be associated with the photo or name. Like defamation, it requires that the person be portrayed negatively and falsely. There can be no false light if the representation is true. If the representation is untrue and a reasonable person would find the reference offensive, there would be a cause of action. For example, if you were to post someone's photograph next to an article about sexually transmitted diseases, that could be considered an invasion of privacy under a false light theory.

This right is only recognized in thirty states because it is so similar to defamation. It should be noted that knowledge of falsity or a reckless disregard for the truth are elements of this claim. In other words, exaggerating in a newsworthy post could result in a cause of action when the publisher of the post knows the exaggerations to be untrue. For example, writing about someone living in abject poverty when you have been to his or her middle-class home could result in a claim for false light.

1.9 WHAT IS A RIGHT OF PUBLICITY?

The right of publicity (also known as commercial appropriation) is the ability to profit from your own name or likeness. It prevents others from using your name or likeness (i.e., a representation of you that can be identified as you) for their commercial benefit. Although it is usually associated with celebrities, every person, regardless of how famous, has a right to prevent unauthorized use of their name or likeness to sell products or services. It has less to do with invasion of privacy and more to do with the economic value of your name and likeness. This is why this type of suit is mostly filed by celebrities (there is an inherent value in our society for their name or likeness). The right of publicity also includes a person's implied endorsement of a product or service. It does not cover the use of names or photos for news reports or other publications of public interest.

1.10 HOW DO I AVOID A LAWSUIT FOR BREACH OF RIGHT TO PUBLICITY?

As mentioned previously, the best defense to an intentional tort is consent. The easiest way to avoid a lawsuit for breach of right of privacy is to obtain releases from anyone whose photo or name you wish to use on your website or blog. If this is not possible, you need to make sure you are not putting this person in a false light, the photo is truthful, and it is newsworthy or otherwise of public interest. If you are using a photo or name for commercial purposes, regardless of whether one is a private individual or celebrity, you will need this person's permission. A release should always be in writing. In some states, the right of publicity can be exercised by the person's estate when the person whose photo or name you wish to use is deceased. In California, for example, the Celebrity Rights Act allows the heirs of a deceased celebrity the right to profit from the celebrity's likeness for seventy years from the date of death.

2   AVOIDING INFRINGEMENT

ISSUES WHEN POSTING CONTENT

I n the 2008 California case of *Disney Enterprises, Inc. v. Showstash.com*,[31] the court entered a judgment of $2.765 million against Showstash.com, which was a website that provided links to movies on third-party websites. These third-party websites contained infringing materials. Even though Showstash.com did not create the infringing material or post the infringing material, it engaged in "*contributory copyright infringement* and inducement of copyright infringement by actively searching *for*, identifying, collecting, posting, organizing, indexing, and *posting . . . links* to infringing material [emphasis added]" according the court.

If you didn't know that you could be found liable for contributory infringement due to links on your site, this case should be a wake-up call. Not only have links been found to give rise to contributory copyright infringement but they could also subject you to direct trademark and copyright infringement lawsuits. This chapter will explain how to avoid some of the legal risks involved in these common practices (such as linking) and other laws with which you will need to comply. It also explains how to legally link to other sites, copy text or images from other sites, forward content via email or Twitter, use registered trademarks that belong to others, and post videos and photographs. It explains what to do if you receive a takedown notice or cease-and-desist letter. It also discusses how a website's terms of use can affect the ownership of the content you post.

2.1 CAN I COPY INFORMATION FROM OTHER WEBSITES IF I LIST THEM AS SOURCES?

It depends on a variety of factors. If you are copying material off the Internet for commercial purposes and placing it on your website or in your post, you will need to obtain the permission of the owner of the material (either through contacting him and obtaining written consent or by locating permission on his website—usually in his terms of use). If you are copying information for noncommercial purposes, you may fall under the so-called fair use exception. In other words, you can copy an image of artwork for an article that discusses or criticizes the work, but you cannot use the same artwork as a background on your website. It is also acceptable to copy material that you know is in the public domain.[32]

The rule of thumb is that material you find on the Internet cannot be copied or republished, even if you source it, without the owner's consent. This is probably the most violated area of law because of how easy it is to copy material off the Internet and because of a misunderstanding of copyright laws. Please note that if you will be using someone else's work for your own commercial purposes, your safest bet is to request permission to use such materials. The No Electronic Theft Act (NET Act) criminally penalizes anyone who willfully infringes on a copyright by electronic means where the value of the copyrighted material exceeds $1,000.[33] There is no reason to subject yourself to this liability when you can create your own work or obtain permission from the copyright owner (if the materials you seek are not in the public domain or your use does not fall within the fair use exception).

Copyright infringement occurs when someone copies someone else's copyrighted work improperly. The first misunderstanding of copyright law is that unless there is a copyright notice, the work is in the public domain. Nothing could be further from the truth. Copyright protection attaches as soon as copyrightable material is placed in fixed form. To determine if infringement exists, assuming there has been no permission granted and the use does not fall within the fair use exception, the court will look to see if the work is "substantially similar" to the original work and that you had access to the original work. Obviously, if the original work is posted on the Internet, it is easy to prove access. In determining whether your use was a fair use under the law, the courts will examine the following: (1) purpose: is it commercial or informational, (2) nature: is it fictional or nonfictional, (3) amount: large versus small amount of original work, and (4) effect on market for original work: does the infringing work compete with the original work in terms of sales?[34]

If the copying is commercial, it is more likely to be found infringing. If the original source is fictional, it is more likely to be found infringing. If a large portion of the original work can be found in your work, it is more likely to be found infringing. If your copying will reduce sales of the original work, it is more likely to be found infringing.

2.2 CAN I COPY WORK THAT IS IN THE PUBLIC DOMAIN?

As mentioned above, just because something is on the Internet and does not have a copyright notice attached, does not mean it is in the public domain. Work that is expressly within the public domain, however, can be copied. Works get entered into the public domain either because they were created that way, produced by the federal government, or because the copyright on them has expired. Despite the fact that most of what is on the Internet cannot be used without the author's permission, there are many works which are in the public domain. If you want to search for items in the public domain, you can check out the Internet Archive website at www.archive.org. You can also visit your local or nearby university library for help on locating such information. Another source is to search for Creative Commons licensed materials at the Creative Commons website, www.creativecommons.com, which has a variety of works you can use. It is important when using the Creative Commons website that you understand the exact nature of the permitted use. It is not all public domain material. Most of it can be used, but you may have to give a certain type of credit or be restricted from using it for commercial purposes. The website explains the different levels of permission authorized by those contributing materials to its website.

2.3 CAN I LINK TO OTHER WEBSITES WITHOUT THEIR CONSENT?

There are a number of reasons why you would want to include links to other websites on your site or blog. That is what makes the Internet the Internet. You can look at one page and find a link to another page, click on it, and immediately find yourself on the new page. You can then click the "back" button and get back to where you were originally. A hypertext link is an underlined phrase or work which, when clicked, will take you to another page either on your website or on someone else's. Although most people would find this activity to merely be of assistance to the user or for the purpose of providing the source of the information you are posting, some courts have found linking to be infringing if the link indicates a relationship between the sites where none exists or if the link is to infringing materials.[35] The general rule is that a link to another site's homepage will probably be acceptable, whereas a link to an internal page (known as deep linking) could be found to be infringing. In *Live Nation Motor Sports, Inc. F/K/A SFX Motor Sports, Inc. v. Robert Davis, D/B/A Tripleclamps and www.supercrosslive.com,*[36] the court held that deep linking to an audio podcast was copyright infringement.

The Digital Millennium Copyright Act specifically references links in Section 512(d). The provision states that an online service provider shall not be held liable for "infringement of copyright by reason of the provider referring or *linking* users to an online location containing infringing material or infringing activity, by using information location tools, including a directory, index, reference, pointer, or hypertext link [emphasis added]." In order to claim this protection, you must have a takedown procedure on your website, not have actual knowledge of the infringement, not receive any financial compensation for the infringing material, and promptly remove the material once notified of the infringement.

If you do use links on your site or in your posts, you should clearly state that your link is not an endorsement of the other site and that you are not responsible for their privacy policy or terms of use. You should check the terms of use of the site that you wish to link to in order to assure yourself that linking will be permitted. You will also want to link to the homepage only (unless you have permission to deep link). In addition, because of the possibility of contributory infringement, you want to make sure you do not link to a site that contains defamatory material or copyright infringing material.

Finally, if a website asks you to remove the link, your safest bet is to comply. While the Digital Millennium Copyright Act provides a "safe harbor" for Internet service providers, you must follow the statute exactly. Keep in mind that there are courts that have found websites with links to infringing materials liable for contributory infringement.

2.4 CAN I FORWARD ARTICLES FROM ONLINE NEWSPAPERS OR MAGAZINES?

Some news sites permit and even encourage users to forward their articles with proper attribution given. However, because newspapers and magazines are copyrighted, unless you fall within the fair use exception described above, forwarding the articles to your clients could be copyright infringement. You will need to examine the legal notices and/or terms of use on the website. If the website itself indicates that you may forward its articles, then you may.

Please note that if the terms indicate that only the entire article may be forwarded, you may not forward less than that. Of course, you will also need to indicate the source of the article and make it clear that it is not your work. Otherwise, you should not copy or email (republish) someone else's material without that person's consent.[37]

2.5 CAN I COPY AND/OR EMAIL REPORTS AND INFORMATION FROM GOVERNMENT WEBSITES?

It depends. Copyright protection does not cover reports and other documents generated by the US government.[38] However, state and local governments generally claim copyright ownership of the works they create. If you copy materials from a US government website that is in the public domain, you should still indicate the source.[39] In order to make sure that the material is in the public domain, you should examine the terms of use at the bottom of the web page. For example, whereas a report prepared by a US government employee is in the public domain, the same report prepared by an independent contractor may not be.

2.6 WHAT LEGAL RISKS ARE THERE IN POSTING A PHOTOGRAPH?

When you are the photographer who took a photograph, you own the copyright to the photograph. For example, if you take a photo of a sunset and use it as part of your background or logo, you can prevent others from copying it. There are different risks when you use a photo that has an identifiable person in it or has been taken by someone else. While many states recognize an individual's right to privacy and the right of publicity, the extent of the right varies significantly from jurisdiction to jurisdiction. See questions 1.7 through 1.10 regarding these rights. You should not post a photograph of anyone that could result in a claim of defamation, false light, invasion of privacy, or public disclosure of private facts. If the photograph is embarrassing or shows the person in a very negative light, you are opening yourself up to a lawsuit. Even if the photograph was taken in a public place with the subject posing for you and is quite flattering, the most prudent course of action is to obtain a release prior to posting the photograph. A release is a binding written agreement consenting to the use of the photograph signed by the subject of the photograph usually in exchange for compensation.

Because of the right of publicity discussed in questions 1.9 and 1.10, people have the right to control the use of their identity. This right permits individuals to profit from the use of their name, photo, or voice in connection with a product or service. There is an exception to this right of publicity in terms of news and other commentary of public interest, but if you are using a photo that is not in the public domain, you will need to obtain a release. If you do not have a written release, a person whose photo or name you used could sue you for violating his or her right to publicity, for defamation, or for a breach of his or her right to privacy, depending on the nature of the photo. This is particularly important when using photographs of celebrities.

A good release is short so that people can easily understand it and has more impact if signed on the spot. Even if your photograph is not defamatory, was taken in a public locale, and is not for a commercial purpose; you probably should still obtain a release.

In the case of a photo taken by someone else, it is the photographer who generally holds the copyright. Prior to using the photo, even if it is of you, you would need to seek permission directly from him or her. When having a photograph professionally taken, you will only receive certain rights to the image. Many photographic studios will inform you that you only have the right to the photos they sell you and that you may not make copies of them in any form. You may be able to purchase the digital rights, which would allow you to post as many copies as you like, but you need to verify this before posting.

2.7 WHAT LEGAL RISKS ARE THERE IN POSTING A VIDEO?

There are a number of legal issues in posting videos online. The first risk involves your exclusive ownership rights when posting a video that you have created on someone else's site. If you post a video to a site that you do not own, like Facebook or YouTube, you are subject to its terms of use. These terms affect the rights you have to your video.

Section 6C of YouTube's terms reads as follows:

> For clarity, you retain all of your ownership rights in your Content. However, by submitting Content to YouTube, you hereby grant YouTube a worldwide, non-exclusive, royalty-free, sublicenseable and transferable license to use, reproduce, distribute, prepare derivative

works of, display, and perform the Content in connection with the Service and YouTube's (and its successors' and affiliates') business, including without limitation for promoting and redistributing part or all of the Service (and derivative works thereof) in any media formats and through any media channels. You also hereby grant each user of the Service a non-exclusive license to access your Content through the Service, and to use, reproduce, distribute, display and perform such Content as permitted through the functionality of the Service and under these Terms of Service. The above licenses granted by you in video Content you submit to the Service terminate within a commercially reasonable time after you remove or delete your videos from the Service. You understand and agree, however, that YouTube may retain, but not display, distribute, or perform, server copies of your videos that have been removed or deleted. The above licenses granted by you in user comments you submit are perpetual and irrevocable.[40]

Section 1 of Facebook's terms reads:

You own all of the content and information you post on Facebook, and you can control how it is shared through your privacy and application settings. In addition:

1. For content that is covered by intellectual property rights, like photos and videos (IP content), you specifically give us the following permission, subject to your privacy and application settings: you grant us a non-exclusive, transferable, sub-licensable, royalty-free, worldwide license to use any IP content that you post on or in connection with Facebook (IP License). This IP License ends when you delete your IP content or your account unless your content has been shared with others, and they have not deleted it.[41]

What is important to understand is that while you retain copyright ownership on both of these sites, you are giving up some rights. You are granting a transferable license to both Facebook and YouTube, which means they can then license your video to others for profit without compensating you. In addition, YouTube reserves the right to create derivative works of your video, meaning it could modify it and republish it.

The second major issue with video is content: identifiable people; music, movies, or other intellectual property in the background; defamatory content; privacy or publicity issues; and pornography. The same issues that apply to text and photographs apply to videos. The main concern is inadvertent copyright infringement because of intellectual property in the background. When Prince found a YouTube video of a toddler dancing to one of his songs, he sued the mother to have it removed, claiming copyright infringement.[42]

2.8 CAN I USE REAL NAMES IN MY BLOG?

This issue goes to right of privacy and right to publicity. See questions 1.7–1.10. In general, it is not a good idea to reveal private information about people. There is a different set of rules for publishing information about people who are public figures.

2.9 HOW DO I AVOID COPYRIGHT INFRINGEMENT?

If you use only the content that you create, you will not infringe on others' copyrights. If you desire to use content that belongs to someone else, you will need to seek written permission. You can also use material that is in the public domain and, to the extent permitted, material under a creative commons license. Otherwise, you must fall within a fair use category. See question 2.1.

With respect to avoiding copyright infringement in terms of what others post on your site, you can claim protection under Section 512(c) of the Digital Millennium Copyright Act (DMCA), which provides that as an Internet service provider you will not be held liable for what others post on your website provided you do not have knowledge of the infringement, have a policy on your website for takedown notices, do not receive financial compensation for the infringing materials, and promptly remove the infringing material upon notice. You must follow the statute exactly to obtain this protection.

2.10 HOW DO I AVOID TRADEMARK INFRINGEMENT?

There are several situations in which you may want to use someone else's trade name: as part of your own name, to discuss something this business did, or as a search engine optimization strategy. Not everyone registers his or her trade name. If you have done research and determined that someone has registered a trade name that you wanted to use, you may want to consider another name. If it is neither federally registered nor registered in your state, you may be able to use it. The court will examine the facts (if someone brings a claim against you) to determine if your use actually constitutes infringement.

In determining whether infringement of a mark has occurred on the Internet, the court will consider the likelihood that a consumer will confuse the products or services. An infringing mark that looks or sounds similar, or relates to goods or services that are similar, is more likely to be found infringing. For example, if someone had already registered Kelly's Teddies for the sale of teddy bears and you start using the name Kelly's Teddies to sell lingerie, the court would be less likely to find infringement than if you were selling some kind of stuffed animal. The infringement could be found, however, if both of the websites were very similar in appearance.

The remedies for infringement can include injunction (preventing the infringer from continuing his or her use of the mark), damages (the amount lost due to the infringement), and the infringer's profits from the wrongful usage (what the infringer made with his or her use would have to be turned over to the plaintiff), and in the event of infringement upon a federally registered mark, treble damages and attorney fees could be awarded in certain cases.

Please note that most domain name registrars do not guarantee that the name you choose is not being used by someone else.[43] It is your responsibility to make sure no one else is using the name you want to use, or if someone is, that you can still use yours. If you do use someone else's name, you will be subject to liability if your actions are in bad faith,[44] but regardless of your intent, if someone else is using and enforcing a trademark, you could be prevented from using your domain name even if the registration is innocent. Please make sure you thoroughly research your name before spending any money on it.

2.11 CAN I EVER USE SOMEONE ELSE'S TRADEMARK WITHOUT THEIR CONSENT?

Sometimes. Not all use of trademarks by non-owners is actionable. You have the fair use right to use someone else's trademark when providing criticism, commentary, news reporting, or other noncommercial expression. In addition, nominative fair use is also permitted. Nominative fair use occurs when you have to use another's trademark to describe your business. For example, if you repair only Dell computers, you would need to be able to advertise that using the trademark "Dell." Nominative use is found when the product or service cannot be identified without the use of the trademark, the user is only using as much of it as necessary, and the user is not suggesting endorsement by the trademark company.

In *Smith v. Wal-Mart Stores, Inc.*,[45] Smith brought an action against Wal-Mart (after being threatened) to declare that his use of the Wal-Mart name and logos on his anti-Wal-Mart website did not violate the megastore's trademarks. Wal-Mart sought to have the offending domain names transferred to it. The court, however, denied the motion, ruling that Smith's uses of Wal-Mart's trademarks were parodies and therefore protected under the fair use copyright doctrine. The court indicated that no one would be confused because no one would believe that Wal-Mart had set up websites criticizing itself.

2.12 WHAT DO I DO IF I RECEIVE A TAKEDOWN NOTICE?

If you own a website and want to be afforded the protection of the Digital Millennium Copyright Act (DMCA), you must follow certain procedures. The DMCA provides immunity from civil and criminal liability to Internet service providers, including website owners, for copyright infringement due to posts made by third parties. This does not protect you from liability for posts made by you, your employees, or your agents. To receive this protection, you are required to post your takedown procedures and a contact person for the takedown notice. It is additionally required that you are not receiving financial compensation for posting the infringing material and that you had no knowledge of the infringement.

If you receive a DMCA takedown notice, you should immediately take the following steps:

1. Remove the offending material.
2. Notify the poster of the material that you have received a takedown notice.
3. Notify the entity sending the takedown notice that you have removed the material.

The DMCA also contains a provision allowing the poster to submit a counter-notice claiming ownership of the offending materials and asking that it be reposted.

In addition, if you believe the original takedown notice was made in bad faith, you can pursue an anti-SLAPP claim (also discussed in question 1.5). Approximately twenty-seven states have anti-SLAPP statutes,[46] which allow the dismissal of lawsuits brought in bad faith. SLAPP is the acronym for "a strategic lawsuit against public participation." It is a lawsuit brought by a plaintiff with the purpose to silence critics by burdening them with the cost of defending a lawsuit against them. The California anti-SLAPP statute[47] allows the defendant in a SLAPP suit to file a motion to dismiss a complaint when it arises from material that is constitutionally protected. If the defendant can show that the claim lacks merit, and the plaintiff cannot show otherwise, not only will the case be dismissed but the defendant may also recover certain attorney fees.

In the case of *Lenz v. Universal Music Corp.*,[48] Universal sent a takedown notice to YouTube regarding a video of a toddler dancing to a Prince song. Lenz, the mother who posted the video, filed a counter-notice asking that the video be reposted as clear fair use. Lenz took the further step of suing Universal under 17 USC Section 512(f), which provides, "Any person who knowingly materially misrepresents under this section that material or activity is infringing. . . shall be liable for any damages, including costs and attorney's fees, incurred by the alleged infringer. . . as the result of the service provider relying upon such misrepresentations in removing or disabling access to the material or active claims to be infringing." As a result, Lenz was able to recover some of her attorney fees.

There has been a recent push for a federal anti-SLAPP law because of the differing results in the different states for a website that operates in all states. The Free Speech Act of 2012[49] was introduced by Senator Jon Kyl (R-AZ) in an effort to curb SLAPP suits that attempt to silence protected speech.

2.13 WHAT DO I DO IF I RECEIVE A CEASE-AND-DESIST LETTER?

A cease-and-desist letter will come from either a person who owns the copyright or this person's attorney. This is different than a takedown notice pursuant to the DMCA. It does not mean you are going to be sued. It just means that someone believes you are infringing on his or her intellectual property.

You need to investigate the claim and then respond. Do not ignore the letter. It will be asking that you either take down the offending material or pay money. If it is asking you to remove the material and you do not have a reason to keep it there, you should probably just remove it. If the letter is asking for money, you need to decide if you want to pay and keep the material posted. (This is called a license fee. When you post intellectual property that belongs to someone else, you should pay for the use.)

If this is something that you posted and you are certain that you own the copyright, that it is in the public domain, or that you have the permission of the actual owner to post it, say so in your response letter and ask for proof that the person owns the intellectual property.[50] If you are not certain as to ownership, you should probably meet with an attorney to discuss before responding.

2.14 WHAT DO I DO IF I GET SUED?

Chances are that, prior to being sued, you will receive either a takedown notice or a demand letter. Most of the lawsuits threatened today are filed by the Recording Industry Association of America (RIAA) and the Motion Picture Association of America (MPAA) and involve the copying for personal use of songs and movies from the Internet. These organizations actively seek out the IP addresses of those who download songs and movies from the Internet. If the actual individual downloading the song or movie is unknown, the organization will then file a John Doe lawsuit against the Internet service provider to obtain the contact information of the alleged infringer. If you are sued, and you have illegally downloaded songs, you will probably want to settle. If you believe your use is not illegal, you should contact an attorney as soon as possible. Defenses include the use of BitTorrent to obtain access to the song, that your downloading was permitted because you already purchased the song or movie, or that your listening to the song was fair use. These, however, are not determinations you should make on your own.

One case that I have been following involves Jammie Thomas-Rasset, who allegedly downloaded twenty-four songs and shared them online. Jammie appears to be one of the few people who have refused to settle with the RIAA. A Minnesota jury found her liable for $1.5 million ($62,500 per song). If this sounds crazy to you, you are not alone. This type of lawsuit did not exist until the Copyright Act was amended in 1997, removing the requirement of financial gain from the definition of infringement. This allowed the RIAA and MPAA to file lawsuits against individuals and claim statutory damages (which are thousands of times larger than the cost of the song or the movie). On September 11, 2012, the Eighth Circuit Court of Appeals reversed the district court's reduction of the award and reinstated the award of $222,000, which was the amount awarded by the jury in the first trial. (She is on her fourth appeal.)

2.15 CAN I BE SUBJECT TO JAIL TIME FOR COPYRIGHT INFRINGEMENT?

Prior to the No Electronic Theft Act of 1997 (NET Act), criminal penalties could only be imposed for copyright infringement if there was a profit motive on the part of the defendant. After the Internet became more popular, people started making music available for download. Since they were doing this for free, there was a loophole in the law. The NET Act changed the copyright infringement law in response to the growth of the Internet by allowing criminal prosecution for noncommercial copyright infringement. Essentially, "the reproduction or distribution, including by electronic means, during any 180-day period, of one or more copies or phonorecords of one or more copyrighted works, which have a total retail value of more than $1,000, shall be punished as provided under section 2319 of title 18." Thus, the sharing of songs, games, software, and movies over the Internet is actually a crime punishable through jail time and a fine. Criminal liability (in addition to civil liability) attaches if your infringement is "willful." Violating the NET Act can result in one to ten years of jail time as well as substantial fines.[51]

Under Section 506(a) of the Copyright Act, copyright infringement is considered criminal if the infringement is willful and either (1) for commercial advantage or financial gain, (2) involves copies with a total retail value over $1,000, or (3) makes an unpublished work publicly available on a computer if that person knew or should have known that the work was intended for commercial distribution. The statute itself does not define "willful," and the courts have not been consistent in determining whether the copying must be intentional. If the *copying* only needs to be done with willful intent, then most copying will be considered criminal. If the government must prove that the defendant knew the copying would violate copyright laws—that the *infringement* was done with willful intent—this higher stand would result in fewer prosecutions. The burden of proof is on the government to show that the infringement is willful. In *United States v. Moran*,[52] the court defined "willful" as meaning "willful intent to infringe." In *United States v. Backer*,[53] the court held that the intent to copy was enough to show willful intent under Section 506. If you know your copying is illegal, you can be prosecuted criminally.[54]

The Intellectual Property Act of 2008[55] also made it easier to prosecute copyright infringement cases by removing the requirement of copyright registration before bringing a criminal charge. It also increased the scope of the act to include additional activities that could subject someone to criminal prosecution.

Another area to be aware of for social media marketers is the CAN-SPAM Act.[56] Spam is typically understood to be unsolicited emails sent out in bulk. While sending out mass emails is not generally a crime, the CAN-SPAM Act makes it "unlawful for any person to initiate the transmission, to a protected computer, of a commercial electronic mail message . . . that is materially false or materially misleading."[57] While most social media marketers have learned to collect emails from those they wish to contact and provide an opt-out option, there are also some additional requirements. First, false or misleading subject lines and headers are not permitted. Second, the sender must be identified and provide a real address in the email. Violating this Act can result in jail time and hefty fines. There have been some significant jail sentences imposed in recent years. In *US v. Kilbride*,[58] the defendants were sentenced to sixty-three months and seventy-eight months, respectively, for sending unsolicited bulk emails regarding adult websites.[59]

It is important to note that although this was not a criminal case, in *Facebook, Inc. v. MaxBounty Inc.*,[60] a federal court applied the CAN-SPAM Act to posts made on Facebook. The court's ruling was based on the language of the CAN-SPAM Act, which applies to "commercial electronic mail messages." This holding has significant implications for those whose marketing efforts center on Facebook postings. Although the case is not a binding precedent, the expansion of the CAN-SPAM Act to Facebook is entirely reasonable and could easily be applied in other courts. As businesses and marketers increase their use of Facebook, it is important to remember that these posts need to comply not only with the CAN-SPAM Act but also to Federal Trade Commission (FTC) and state advertising regulations and the terms of use of any social media sites on which they send out mass communications.

3 ADVERTISING LAWS AND
OTHER GOVERNMENTAL REGULATIONS

On March 15, 2011, the FTC reported that it completed its first investigation and enforcement activity under the new FTC Endorsement Guides[61] prohibiting false advertising on the Internet. Essentially, the FTC Endorsement Guides provide that when someone posts a positive review of a service or product and that person is either connected to the seller or receives some sort of compensation for the positive review, the "material connection" between the reviewer and the seller of the product or service must be disclosed. In this case, Legacy Learning, a company that provides guitar lessons on DVDs, had an affiliate review program that compensated bloggers and other online publishers for posting positive reviews about its program. Because those posting the reviews did not reveal that they were compensated, as required under the Endorsement Guides, the company agreed to settle the action with the FTC and pay a $250,000 penalty for its violation of the Endorsement Guides.[62]

Even though these Endorsement Guides went into effect January 1, 2010, there are still many companies out there with these types of affiliate programs. Because both the endorser and the company can be found liable under the act, this issue is important to both social media marketers and those utilizing social media. Social media is a powerful tool and is being regularly used for advertising purposes. What makes it so powerful is the ability of a single message to go viral in a very short amount of time. While this can be an enormous boon for those benefiting from a positive message, it can be devastating for those who are being negatively portrayed. The main problem is that unlike traditional advertising, in which the company originates the message, with social media the company has little control over the content and flow of messages generated by users of social media (i.e., user-generated content or UGC).

This chapter will explain not only the new FTC rules, but also some other governmental regulations that could result in liability for unsuspecting social media marketers. Even though a social media marketer may not be manufacturing or selling products or services, he or she may still have liability under federal and state advertising and consumer fraud statutes. This chapter also describes the laws relating to contests, customer services issues, and the obligation to correct false or misleading posts. It gives an overview of the types of laws that may be applicable and how the laws of another state or foreign country could potentially have an impact on what is posted.

3.1 WHAT LIMITS ARE THERE ON MY RIGHT TO ADVERTISE ON MY WEBSITE?

The same rules that apply to traditional advertising will generally apply to online advertising. The two main federal statutes that apply to marketing/advertising are the Federal Trade Commission Act (FTC Act) and the Lanham Act. Additionally, there are state consumer fraud statutes, defamation laws,[63] and false advertising statutes.[64] Please note that almost any statement that is intended to draw attention to a particular product or service can be considered advertising. Social media marketing is usually considered advertising. While advertising laws were meant to protect consumers from bad conduct by businesses, their applicability to user generated content can be problematic for both business and social media marketers.

Section 5 of the FTC Act makes unfair and deceptive trade practices illegal. Marketers using social media to project their message must make sure the statements they make about services or products are truthful, fair, and not misleading. They must also be substantiated. Consumers tend to hold user-generated content in higher regard than statements made by the companies themselves. While a company cannot control everything that is said about it on a social media site, it can be subject to liability when it solicits user-generated content that turns out to violate the FTC Act or other laws. If you have created a business page on Facebook, you should monitor the postings there and remove the ones that could result in a lawsuit.

With respect to making statements about your or someone else's products or services, honesty and full disclosure are the best policies. This means you need to provide the consumer with enough information to make an informed choice, including price and warnings. You must also be able to substantiate any claims made about the benefits of the products.

Section 43(a) of the Lanham Act prohibits false and misleading advertising regarding a company's own products or those of its competitors. In *Northern Star Industries, Inc. v. Douglas Dynamics LLC*,[65] a federal judge granted the plaintiff's request for a preliminary injunction against the defendant under the Lanham Act. The defendant, a competitor of the plaintiff, created a series of advertisements leading consumers to believe that using the plaintiff's snowplow would cause personal injury whereas the defendant's own snowplows would not. Some of these advertisements appeared on the defendant's Facebook page. The court found these representations to be false and took the unusual step of ordering the defendant to post a corrective ad stating the truth on Facebook (in addition to granting the preliminary injunction preventing the defendant from making further false claims). It appears that the judge recognized the reach of social media campaigns and wanted to make sure her remedy fit the violation.

There are also some links regarding advertising on the Small Business Administration (SBA) website at http://www.sba.gov/content/how-comply-with-advertising-laws and state consumer protection departments at www.consumeraction.gov/state.shtml. The FTC website also contains a guide to advertising on the Internet at www.ftc.gov/bcp/edu/pubs/business/ecommerce/bus28.shtm.

3.2 CAN A PERSON OR ENTITY THAT POSTS CONTENT REGARDING SOMEONE ELSE'S PRODUCTS OR SERVICES BE LIABLE FOR INJURIES CAUSED BY SUCH PRODUCTS OR SERVICES?

While most actions by the FTC involve failure to mention a material connection with respect to product endorsements, under the FTC Endorsement Guides, an endorser can also be held liable for false and unsubstantiated claims. Section 255.1(d) of the FTC's Endorsement Guides[66] indicates that endorsers can be held liable "for statements made in the course of their endorsement."

The FTC Endorsement Guides specifically apply to bloggers but would logically extend to anyone who makes online posts about a product or service. Product liability for those endorsing a product is most commonly applied when the endorser is known as an expert and is compensated for endorsing products.[67] The rule here is to always disclose your material relationship with the manufacturer or seller of the product you are endorsing and to avoid making false or unsubstantiated claims about a product.

The bigger issue is the liability that attaches to the seller or manufacturer for claims made on the Internet by those who receive compensation for endorsing the products or otherwise have a material connection to the seller or manufacturer, such as being employees. This liability would reach the seller or manufacturer even if the employee made the post on a social networking site without the knowledge of the employer. As a social media marketer, you have an obligation when acting on behalf of a business to make sure that those posting about the company comply with the FTC Endorsement Guides.

If you are a seller or manufacturer of a product or service and you have begun an affiliate program in order to generate "buzz" about your product or service through social networking sites, there are certain steps you will need to take in order to avoid an action by the FTC. First, you should use written affiliate agreements outlining the requirements on your affiliates in order to comply with the FTC Endorsement Guides. You should have an express provision requiring your affiliates to agree to comply with all federal and state laws (including advertising and consumer protection laws). The agreement should require affiliates to disclose their relationship with you as an affiliate and expressly agree to comply with the CAN-SPAM Act (including a prohibition of bulk emails on your behalf or about your product).[68]

It should be noted that not only can the endorser be liable for the unsubstantiated claims it makes but the company selling or manufacturing the product or service can also be liable for unsubstantiated claims made by an endorser.[69] Example 5 of the FTC Endorsement Guides states:

> A skin care products advertiser participates in a blog advertising service. The service matches up advertisers with bloggers who will promote the advertiser's products on their personal blogs. The advertiser requests that a blogger try a new body lotion and write a review of the product on her blog. Although the advertiser does not make any specific claims about the lotion's ability to cure skin conditions and the blogger does not ask the advertiser whether there is substantiation for the claim, in her review the blogger writes that the lotion cures eczema and recommends the product to her blog readers who suffer from this condition. *The advertiser is subject to liability for misleading or unsubstantiated representations made through the blogger's endorsement* [emphasis added].[70]

3.3 HOW DO THE NEW FTC ENDORSEMENT GUIDES AFFECT THOSE POSTING CONTENT ONLINE?

As discussed in question 3.1, the same rules that apply to traditional advertising, including consumer fraud statutes, defamation laws,[71] and false advertising statutes,[72] will generally apply to online advertising. Please note that almost any statement that is intended to draw attention to a particular product or service can be considered advertising. Although advertising is generally regulated by the Federal Trade Commission (FTC), there are many other industry-specific agencies and their state counterparts.[73]

The FTC recently updated its Guide Concerning the Use of Endorsements and Testimonials in Advertising effective December 1, 2009,[74] which concerns testimonials and endorsements on websites and blogs. Going forward, if you (or a user on your blog or website) represent results from the use of a product or service as typical when that is not the case, you will need to also disclose the results that most consumers can expect. This is different from the previous FTC guide, which allowed advertisers to use extremely positive results in a testimonial as long as they included the disclaimer such as "these results are not typical." In addition, the revised guide also requires that the relationship between a supplier of the product or services and the endorser be disclosed. For example, if a blogger recommends a product on his blog that he received for free or was paid to discuss on his blog, the blogger is required to disclose this information in the blog. Similarly, if an employee recommends a product or service on a discussion board or blog, the employee is required to disclose that he or she is employed by the manufacturer or supplier of the service.[75] The revised guide seems to indicate that both endorsers and advertisers could be liable under the FTC Act for statements they make in an endorsement. This would include false or unsubstantiated statements *and* the failure to disclose a material connection between the advertiser and endorser. As discussed in question 3.2, with respect to making statements about your or someone else's products or services, honesty and full disclosure are the best policies.

The effect of the FTC Endorsement Guides is that both the company and the person making the post can be held liable for failing to disclose their "arrangement." An arrangement can include the supplying of free products, compensation for mentioning products, or that the reviewer is an employee of the company. To "disclose" means that the arrangement is conspicuously made so that the consumer knows the nature of the relationship between the reviewer and the company. You cannot just make a general statement on your website that you review products for companies or that you are an affiliate to companies. The disclosure must be specific to the product or service you are reviewing. The most important piece of this requirement is that your post must not include "misleading or unsubstantiated representations." If you have never tried the product or service and write about it, that post would be unsubstantiated.

In the case of *Legacy Learning* discussed in the introduction, failing to disclose that the reviewers of the product were receiving compensation result-ed in Legacy having to pay a penalty of $250,000 (as a result of settlement discussions).

3.4 WHO OWNS THE CONTENT THAT I POST ABOUT SOMEONE ELSE'S PRODUCTS OR SERVICES?

There are several issues presented by this question. First, photographs and videos that you post on social media sites are still owned by you, but the terms of use of these sites will give the site owner the right to use what you post for his or her own financial gain. This is allowed because you are express-ly granting them a license to use your intellectual property when you post on their sites. Instagram made this quite clear in its revised terms of use, and consumers created quite a backlash, apparently not realizing that they already granted Facebook and YouTube these rights.[76] Although Instagram eventually relented on the wording, it is doubtful that its business model will change. Social media sites are out there to make money. They are not not-for-profit organizations dedicated to creating forums for you to communicate with your friends and share information.

The second issue in terms of posting about another's products or services is whether or not you are infringing on another's trademarks. As questions 2.10 and 2.11 discussed, you may not use someone else's intellectual prop-erty for your own financial gain; you may only include someone's trademark in your content if you fall within the fair use exception to trademark infringe-ment. If you are infringing on someone's intellectual property, it is not a matter of who owns the post; it is the ability of the intellectual property owner to force you to remove the post.

If you create content within the fair use exception about someone else's intellectual property, it belongs to you. There are additional issues, aside from ownership, when you are posting about someone else's business, product, or service. If you are reviewing a product or service, while this may not be infringement, you will need to make sure you comply with the FTC Endorsement Guides and consumer protection and advertising laws. You will also need to make sure you are not engaging in product disparagement (which is like defamation but applies to a business, product, or service).

There has been a spate of lawsuits regarding reviews made on Yelp. This issue involves reviews that actually result in a loss of business for a company. There is an enormous incentive to have the negative reviews removed. If the reviews are made by a competitor or by a consumer with no knowledge of the product or service being reviewed, the company should be able to force the takedown of the review. However, it is not so clear-cut. First, the website will generally have immunity under the CDA for such posts, but the person who posted the review does not.

What these lawsuits come down to is whether or not a case for defamation or tortious interference with business exists. You do have the right to make a truthful negative review on a website. You do not have the right to remain anonymous or to post false reviews. In *Becker v. Hooshmand*,[77] the case settled out of court for an undisclosed amount resulting from a lawsuit brought by a doctor in Florida against a defendant in Pennsylvania who made allegedly defamatory posts regarding the doctor online. The court also ordered the defendant to stop making further defamatory posts. In *Townson v. Liming*,[78] a Texas judge ordered the defendant to stop making defamatory posts against a doctor whom the defendant had never even seen.

While these cases involved actual wrongdoing on the part of the defendant, it should be noted that if your state does not have an anti-SLAPP statute and you are sued for a negative review, even if you win, you will still have to pay an attorney to defend you. You should always make sure that your reviews are truthful and substantiated. In addition, it is a bad idea to make negative posts regarding a competitor, especially if you fail to disclose that you are a competitor.

The third issue involves ownership of social media pages and names. In *PhoneDog v. Kravitz*,[79] the company sued a former employee, indicating that it owned the Twitter followers to the Twitter handle that was created while the employee was employed at PhoneDog. Although the judge refused to dismiss the case (indicating that PhoneDog was not completely off-base in making such a claim), it ultimately settled out of court.[80] There will be more cases like these as companies realize the value of such accounts. As discussed in Chapter 5, this is one of the reasons why companies need to create social media policies for their employees and agents.

3.5 CAN THE OWNER OR MANUFACTURER OF THE PRODUCT OR SERVICES EDIT WHAT I POST?

As discussed in the answer to question 3.4, you first need to determine if you are violating the company's trademark rights or if you fall into a fair use exception. If you fall within the exception, the owner or manufacturer cannot edit what you post. However, if you are an employee of the owner or manufacturer, different rules may apply. In addition, if you have an affiliate agreement with the manufacturer or seller of the product, you would need to comply with your contract, which may contain language allowing the company to edit what you post or ask you to remove it.

Again, the bigger issue is the potential for tort liability for what you post about another's products or services.

Because a manufacturer or seller of products or services can potentially be liable for comments you make about its product or services, it has a vested interest in preventing false statements from appearing on the Internet. If you do not comply with a cease-and-desist order, it can send a takedown notice to the Internet service provider under either the CDA or the DMCA, asking that the post be removed. Prior to the advent of the Internet, the manufacturer or seller of products or services had direct control of its advertising. Because of the potential for liability for false claims, it must monitor what is being said about it on the Internet. In addition to affiliate arrangements of which it has knowledge, it must also monitor comments made by consumers (and social media marketers). Relationships must be disclosed under the FTC Endorsement Guides, and statements must be substantiated. This means that the seller or manufacturer has a duty to stop false, misleading, or unsubstantiated claims from going viral on the Internet.

The FTC states in "Guides Concerning the Use of Endorsements and Testimonials" (16 CFR Part 255):

> In order to limit its potential liability, the advertiser should ensure that the advertising service provides guidance and training to its bloggers concerning the need to ensure that statements they make are truthful and substantiated. The advertiser should also monitor bloggers who are being paid to promote its products and take steps necessary to halt the continued publication of deceptive representations when they are discovered. If the blogger refuses to disclose sponsorship, or to correct unsubstantiated or misleading statements, then the

advertiser should sever relations with the blogger and not provide further compensation.

3.6 WHAT ARE THE RULES INVOLVING CONTESTS AND PROMOTIONS?

Sweepstakes, contests, and lotteries are governed by federal and state law. Many companies use contests as a way to attract new customers. The difference between sweepstakes, contests, and lotteries is important because if you do not comply with the law regarding the type of promotion you are holding, you could be subject to criminal prosecution. Sweepstakes award prizes based on chance. Contests award prizes based on skill. Lotteries are generally illegal unless run by a state. A lottery is a game of chance that costs money to enter.[81] Sweepstakes are generally legal. If you require something in order for an entrant to participate, such as an entry fee, required purchase, or a significant expenditure of effort, your sweepstakes could be viewed as a lottery, which is illegal in all fifty states and prohibited by the federal government.

Although lotteries may be run by the government, any social media promotion that is considered a lottery is illegal. While games of chance are permissible as sweepstakes, requiring consideration of the entrant is not. States differ as to whether online sweepstakes are illegal lotteries, but there are a couple of measures you can take to reduce the chance that your online contest will be illegal. First, always offer an alternate means of entry. In other words, even though the purpose of the contest may be to capture emails, you should also allow an entrant to send in a postcard with his or her contact information. Both the online entries and the postcard entries must have the same opportunity to win. Some states prohibit any contest where chance is a factor if consideration is also required.

A contest, which requires skill, may require an entry fee and will not be considered an illegal lottery. The key is that there should be no element of chance (as in sweepstakes). Because some states prohibit any entrance fee for a contest, you should first determine what your promotion is (lottery, sweepstakes, or contest) and exclude entrants from states that prohibit these types of contests. If you are holding an online contest, you must exclude entrants from states with requirements that would make your contest illegal.

After you have ascertained that your sweepstakes or contest will meet the legal requirements of the states in which you plan to hold the contest, you will need to provide a set of official rules. The rules must comply with each state's requirements, including statements such as "no purchase is necessary to enter" or "void where prohibited by law." In addition, there are some states that require registration prior to holding a contest or sweepstakes.[82] The rules are important because they serve as a contract between the entrants and the promoter.

The rules should be easily found on the promoter's website. They must include a description of the number and type of prizes, the odds of winning, restrictions on who may enter (if excluding residents of certain states or non-US residents), the retail value of prizes, the date by which entries must be received, the date by which the prizes will be awarded, the name and address of the promoter, a statement that the winner is responsible for taxes on the prizes, a statement that no purchase is necessary, a statement that the sweepstakes or contest is void where prohibited by law, what law governs any disputes, and how a list of winners can be obtained. Some states have additional disclosure requirements.[83]

Some states require that information on your promotion must be kept for a period of time (usually two years) following the promotion. This would include the contest rules and winners.

It is a good idea to consult with an attorney specializing in contests (or whose primary clients are retailers) in order to make sure that your promotion does not run afoul of the law. Do not forget that social media promotions are subject to the same laws as any other promotion. Make sure your promotion does not require an entry fee or purchase. Do not copy another website's official rules thinking that they probably comply with the law. First of all, you do not know whether or not they were prepared by an attorney, and secondly, they may describe a set of circumstances that are different from those that apply to your promotion.

You also need to investigate whether or not the social media site on which you wish to hold your promotion permits such posts and, if so, what rules it has. Facebook, for example, has its own set of rules.[84] Facebook requires certain disclosures to be made and that the promotion uses a third-party application; it also prohibits you from using Facebook's Like button as an entry, among other things. Google+, on the other hand, completely prohibits promotions to be run on a Google+ page. To conduct a promotion through Twitter or YouTube, you must comply with their rules.[85]

Running promotions can be a risky proposition, so you will want to obtain legal counsel before engaging in these types of activities.

3.7 WHAT IS INSTANTANEOUS CUSTOMER SERVICE, AND WHAT ARE THE RISKS?

Instantaneous customer service is a marketing concept that developed due to the Internet. Never before have companies been able to respond to customer complaints and issues instantaneously. These interactions can be facilitated through dedicated websites, social media sites, and Twitter. A possible concern is that you may have employees giving advice or making claims without knowing the legal risks involved. Gone are the days when a marketing manager oversaw all corporate communications. These duties are being delegated to many lower-level employees.

If you are permitting employees or independent contractors to respond to claims made online about your products or services, you need to provide them with a list of rules and procedures outlining what they can and cannot say online. Remember, the FTC Act requires advertisements to be truthful (not misleading), substantiated, and fair. A company can be held vicariously liable for the postings of its employees.

3.8 DO I HAVE AN OBLIGATION TO CORRECT FALSE OR MISLEADING POSTS?

If you created the false or misleading post, it would serve you to correct it in case such post could create injury to another (such as defamation). Keep in mind that if others have already copied or retweeted your post or otherwise forwarded an actionable material that you created, you most likely will not be able to completely erase it from the Internet. This is the risk with online posting. A statement made in haste can cause a great deal of liability because of the ability for it to spread like wildfire. See Chapter 2 regarding tort claims to which you could be subject for your posts. Also, keep in mind that retraction statutes do not provide immunity; they just help mitigate your damages.

If you operate a blog that allows others to post comments, your liability could depend on whether you have a policy permitting you to edit posts or not. See question 1.6 regarding vicarious liability.

3.9 WHAT CONSUMER FRAUD LAWS APPLY TO SOCIAL MEDIA?

Both federal and state consumer fraud laws apply to posts made online. As mentioned in question 3.1, the two most important federal statutes are the

FTC Act and the Lanham Act. The FTC Act prohibits "unfair or deceptive acts or practices" that are "likely to cause substantial injury to consumers."[86] Section 5 of the FTC Act applies to false or misleading statements made to consumers and requires advertisements to be substantiated and fair. The Lanham Act prohibits "false or misleading representation of fact" about their own or another's goods, services, or activities.[87]

Section 5 of the FTC Act states that "unfair methods of competition in or affecting commerce, and unfair or deceptive acts or practices in or affecting commerce, are hereby declared unlawful." At the federal level, the FTC actively enforces its regulations (there is no private cause of action under Section 5 of the FTC Act). Most states have their own consumer fraud statutes, and many of them not only permit state action against violators but also give a right of a private cause of action to those harmed by the false statements or fraud.

A number of lawsuits have been brought as a result of company-sponsored social media campaigns under the Lanham Act. In 2006, Subway sued Quiznos for its involvement in encouraging consumers to upload videos negatively portraying Subway sandwiches.[88] Although the case ultimately settled, the court did not grant Quiznos Motion for Summary Judgment on the grounds that the website owner was not immune from lawsuit under the CDA (which gives website owners immunity from suits involving user-generated content). In other words, it is likely that a company that encourages false and misleading videos to be uploaded about a competitor could be held liable under the Lanham Act.

Interestingly, in Australia, the government agency responsible for enforcing consumer fraud laws has indicated that comments made on Facebook are subject to the same laws as advertisements.[89] This will require companies with Facebook pages to carefully monitor what is being posted on these pages by consumers.

3.10 WHICH STATE'S LAWS APPLY TO MY POSTS?

Your posts and online activities can be viewed in all states. It is not possible, for example, for you to prevent your website from being viewed by the residents of California. The issue is whether or not you have the "minimum contacts" with a particular state to be brought into court there.[90] In order to be subject to personal jurisdiction in a state in which you do not live, you must be able to be reached under that state's "long-arm" statute. Generally, you have to "purposefully avail yourself" to the benefits of being present in or doing business in that state. If this standard is met, the court will weigh the burdens on the defendant to have to defend itself in that state with the interest in the plaintiff seeking relief. While most courts have held that merely having a website is not enough to subject you to another state's long-arm jurisdiction, the courts differ as to how much activity in the state will subject you to it.

In *Cybersell, Inc. v. Cybersell, Inc.*,[91] the court held that the mere presence of a website on the Internet alone will not constitute the "minimum contacts" needed to subject a person to the jurisdiction of every court in every state. "Something more" is needed: either interactivity between the website and the viewers or purposeful marketing in that state. The factors courts look at include commercial versus noncommercial involvement as well as how much interaction there is between the users of the site and the owner. In addition, if marketing is targeted to a specific state, the court will be more likely to find that sufficient contacts exist.

In *Zippo Manufacturing v. Zippo Dot Com, Inc.*,[92] the defendant's website required address information from the users of its news service. The court where the suit was filed found that sufficient to allow the court in the state where the plaintiff was located to obtain jurisdiction over the defendant. Whether or not you can be subject to a state's long-arm statute will depend on the laws of that state and your activities within that state. Well-crafted terms of use[93] indicating that venue and choice of law in your own state will help alleviate some of the risk in doing businesses online, but judgment will ultimately be up to the court in the state in which you are being sued.

3.11 DO I NEED TO BE CONCERNED WITH LAWS IN FOREIGN COUNTRIES?

There is no dispute that the laws of other countries can be very different from the laws in the United States. One of the issues regarding the Internet is that even if you have never left the United States, posts that you make on the Internet can be viewed virtually anywhere in the world. Foreign governments have the right to prosecute those who violate their laws anywhere in the world. While the United States will determine whether or not to extradite you for your alleged crimes, it is probably not a good idea to visit a country where you have been prosecuted in absentia. The United States is currently investigating whether or not to prosecute Wikileaks founder Julian Assange for violations of United States laws despite his location outside the United States.[94]

In terms of jurisdiction, the standard is much higher in an international lawsuit to establish jurisdiction over a United States citizen than it is for one state to establish jurisdiction over the resident of another state. However, some countries have successfully obtained jurisdiction over United States businesses for conduct violating the laws of their country. In the case of *Dow Jones & Co., Inc. v. Gutnick*,[95] the High Court of Australia held that the Australian court had jurisdiction over a United States company that posted a defamatory article about an Australian citizen on the Internet. The online version of the magazine had 550,000 international subscribers and captured 1,700 Australian-based credit cards. The right to sue in Australia was based on the defendant's right to sue where he was harmed. The court indicated that those who "utilize the infrastructure" of another country must comply with the laws in it. Dow Jones ultimately settled the dispute for $580,000.[96]

There are also international laws regarding intellectual property that are also applicable to your online conduct. The United States is party to the Berne Convention, the Universal Copyright Convention, and the Agreement on Trade Related Aspects of International Property Rights (TRIPS Agreement). The Berne Convention protects the intellectual property of the signatory parties. This means that the United States must recognize the copyrights of works originating in other countries to the extent to which it recognizes its own. Under the Universal Copyright Convention, any formality in a country's intellectual property law can be met by the use of the symbol © (C in a circle) accompanied by the year of first publication and the name of the copyright owner (example: © 2013 Kimberly A. Houser). The TRIPS Agreement sets forth the minimum standard copyright protections that a country must have in order to be a member. It also requires enforcement of these standards.

4 PRIVACY LAWS AND SECURITY ISSUES

In 2011, the US Department of Health and Human Services (HHS) Office for Civil Rights (OCR) fined Cignet Health $4.3 million for violating the Health Insurance Portability and Accountability Act (HIPAA) Privacy Rule, the maximum penalty permitted by law.[97] Although part of the penalty was due to Cignet's failure to permit its patients online access to their medical records, the great majority of it was due to Cignet's willful neglect in responding to the HHS's complaint and discovery requests.

The warning here: The government takes privacy violations seriously. You really need to understand and comply with these laws on any site you set up, whether it be your business website, an informational website, or a blog. These laws include the Privacy Act, Freedom of Information Act, Gramm-Leach-Bliley Act, Fair and Accurate Credit Transactions Act, Fair Credit Reporting Act, Health Insurance Portability and Accountability Act, Family Educational Rights and Privacy Act, Driver's Privacy Protection Act, Children's Online Privacy Protection Act, Electronic Communications Privacy Act, the Video Privacy Protection Act, as well as all the state privacy and security breach statutes.[98]

Chapter 4 details some of the issues involving Internet privacy and security. Although the greatest risk falls on those with their own websites, there are many privacy and security issues that can affect those posting content on social media and other sites. This chapter describes the most important privacy laws, how a site's terms and conditions can affect postings, and the need to secure certain information when engaging in social media marketing—especially when the marketer is collecting information from consumers.

4.1 DO I HAVE TO COMPLY WITH HIPAA IF I'M NOT A DOCTOR?

The purpose of the Health Insurance Portability and Accountability Act[99] is to protect consumers' health information. When HIPAA originally came out, the extent of its applicability outside the medical profession ("covered entities") was unclear. The passage of the Health Information Technology for Economic and Clinical Health Act (HITECH), which amended HIPAA, expressly extended the privacy and security obligations to entities with access to consumers' health information. What this means is if your business puts you in contact with the health information of others, you must ensure its security and confidentiality. Depending on what types of businesses you work with, you could be considered a covered "business associate." A "business associate" must also have a procedure for assisting a covered entity in responding to a patient's inquiries, and take measures to ensure the security and integrity of the personal identifiable information (PII) to which they have access as part of their work for the covered entities. Violations of HIPAA and HITECH can result in both civil and criminal penalties. Although the level of security you must provide is unclear, if you are transferring health information, you should at the very least use encrypted email.

The purpose of HITECH is to "enable health information to follow a patient wherever it is needed." The HHS Office of the National Coordinator for Health Information Technology (ONC) and the HHS OCR are responsible for enforcing the privacy laws regarding HITECH. They have made a number of recommendations that would probably be applicable for any entity governed by privacy statutes and any marketer collecting personally identifiable information. These are very good guidelines for the protection of information kept on mobile devices, including phones and laptops.[100] According to the OCR and ONC, the major risks pertaining to mobile devices involve the loss or theft of a mobile device, malware infecting a mobile device, the lending of a mobile device to someone without authorization to view confidential information, and the use of unsecured Wi-Fi networks. Best practices require that you keep personal mobile devices separate from business mobile devices. In other words, it is not a good idea to allow an employee to store confidential information on their personal laptop or phone. Both firewalls and antivirus software on any devices containing confidential information should be installed and frequently updated. The www.healthit. gov website also lists twenty steps which can be tailored to any entity desiring to utilize mobile devices in its businesses.[101]

The OCR recently took action against a hospice that lost a laptop with patient information on it. Hospice of Northern Idaho (HONI) agreed to settle with the OCR after it was discovered that a lost laptop contained information on some 441 patients. The hospice agreed to pay a $50,000 fine. The settlement agreement entered in December 2012 indicated that the hospice failed to meet privacy and security standards in that:

(A) HONI did not conduct an accurate and thorough analysis of the risk to the confidentiality of ePHI on an on-going basis as part of its security management process from the compliance date of the Security Rule to January 17, 2012. In particular, HONI did not evaluate the likelihood and impact of potential risks to the confidentiality of electronic PHI maintained in and transmitted using portable devices, implement appropriate security measures to address such potential risks, document the chosen security measures and the rationale for adopting those measures, and maintain on an on-going basis reasonable and appropriate security measures.

(B) HONI did not adequately adopt or implement security measures sufficient to ensure the confidentiality of ePHI that it created, maintained, and transmitted using portable devices to a reasonable and appropriate level from the compliance date of the Security Rule to May 1, 2011.[102]

What this means is that the hospice did not use reasonable measures to keep patient information secure. You might say that losing a laptop is unlikely, but the real issue is that the nurses use the laptops to do their work in the field. As such, it would be impossible to create a rule disallowing patient information to be kept on mobile devices. As privacy and security law develops, we will hopefully have more guidance as to what exact measures entities can take against privacy and security breaches. For more information see www.HealthIT.gov/mobiledevices.

4.2 DO I HAVE TO COMPLY WITH THE CHILDREN'S ONLINE PRIVACY PROTECTION ACT IF I DON'T DIRECT MY SITE TO CHILDREN?

The age of your users will impact the notices required on your site. According to FTC regulations regarding the Children's Online Privacy Protection Act (COPPA),[103] a website must get a parent's permission for children under the age of thirteen to disclose information. COPPA deals with the use, collection, and disclosure of children's personal information. There are also issues with respect to users under the age of eighteen. Because of state contract law, children under the age of eighteen may not be bound to contracts such as your website user agreement and purchase contracts in certain states. The FTC also regulates advertising and other content directed at children.

Children under the age of thirteen are frequent users of the Internet and mobile devices. Because of their age, their privacy is extremely important. COPPA prohibits the "collection" of PII from children without "prior verifiable parental consent." Under COPPA, "personally identifiable" information includes names, email addresses, home addresses, and phone numbers. "Collection" includes the use of any interactive elements of websites, including posts, photo sharing, and filling out online forms. "Prior verifiable parental consent" means that the parents must be given the option to prevent the disclosure of their children's information to third parties.

The FTC enforces COPPA and can impose civil penalties against those violating it. COPPA applies to websites for children (games and educational) and any other website that is aware that it is collecting information from children. While most educational and game websites expect children to utilize the site, the main legal issues come into play with websites used by the general public in which children may be interested. If a website asks its users for their age, it will be presumed to have actual knowledge of underage users. In addition, if a general website has a children's area, COPPA will also apply.

Because of the advances in smartphone technology, children are now able to access the Internet from their phone. Many mobile apps targeting children (games and educational) do not comply with COPPA, because they do not verify the age of the child or obtain verifiable parental consent to the child's use of the app.[104] With the new trend towards making websites available on mobile phones, social media marketers should ensure that all privacy protections are included on such mobile sites and apps. Earlier in 2012, the FTC conducted an investigation of 400 randomly selected apps on phones that were directed to children under the age of thirteen. The report they issued after the investigation indicated that the developers of apps were routinely "failing to adequately disclose their data practices on their app store pages and the first page ("landing page") of their websites prior to parents and users downloading the apps.[105]

As a result of these findings, in December 2012 the FTC amended COPPA to include "photo, video, and audio files, geolocation information, and persistent identifiers (such as IP addresses or mobile device serial numbers)."[106] The changes also require websites with links to social media sites (plug-ins) to obtain verifiable parental consent before collecting personal information from children under the age of thirteen and add geo-location information to the definition of PII.[107]

4.3 DO I HAVE TO COMPLY WITH THE GRAMM-LEACH-BLILEY ACT IF I'M NOT A BANK?

The Gramm-Leach-Bliley Act (GLBA)[108] mandates specific reporting and disclosure requirements to ensure the financial privacy of customers. It also limits the financial institution's ability to disclose collected information to third parties.[109] When a customer opts out, the financial institution still has the ability to share the customer's information with those who provide services for the financial institution. The act does prevent these affiliates receiving opt-out financial information from disclosing nonpublic, personal information unless the disclosure would be lawful if made directly by the financial institution. Please note that "financial institution" is defined very broadly, and you may want to consult with an attorney if you are unsure of whether it applies to you. According to the FTC, it applies to "non-bank mortgage lenders, loan brokers, some financial or investment advisers, tax preparers, providers of real estate settlement services, and debt collectors."[110] It also applies to third parties (including marketers) who receive such information from financial institutions.

The act requires those covered to provide consumers with annual notices regarding the collection and disclosure of nonpublic private information about the consumer and give the consumers an opportunity to opt out of the disclosures to third parties, and it also requires that PII be kept secure and confidential. The FTC is the enforcement agent for the GLBA. Failure to prevent third parties from accessing the information (even if they are accessing it illegally) can result in an action by the FTC.

Again, your safest bet is to include a privacy policy on your website, comply with it, and take reasonable measures to secure the safety of your clients' private information. Failure to do so could result in violations of both state and federal laws, and in private lawsuits by those affected.

4.4 ARE THERE ANY RULES ON SETTING UP A FORUM?

An Internet forum is an online discussion board usually centered on a specific topic where users can post comments to each other. While some are monitored, many are not. If you have a forum on your website, you should provide terms of use. You will want to prevent users from posting pornographic, defamatory, or infringing materials. In addition, you will want to include a disclaimer indicating that the posts do not reflect the views of the website and that you are not liable for what others post.[111] If you have the time, you can set up the forum in such way that posts have to be approved before being seen online. Some lawyers advise against monitoring your site so that you can truthfully say you were unaware of any violations, while others suggest that monitoring is the better way to know what's on your site and be able to remove it promptly. Regardless, you should make sure you comply with the Digital Millennium Copyright Act and the Communications Decency Act.[112]

4.5 DO STATES HAVE PRIVACY LAWS?

In addition to the constitutional right of privacy and state law regarding personal privacy rights, there are many concerns regarding the privacy of information transmitted over the Internet. Consumers and businesses alike are uncertain about the security of email transmission, the safety of credit card information when making online purchases, the ability of companies to monitor your browsing history, and the use by websites of your personal information. As mentioned previously, federal law regulates specific industries with respect to privacy regulations. There is no general federal law regarding the privacy of data transmitted over the Internet. Most states, however, do regulate this area.

The California Online Privacy Protection Act[113] was the first state law in the nation requiring websites and online service providers to post a privacy policy. Although most other states do not require a posted privacy policy, approximately forty-four states have privacy laws that attempt to safeguard the information of consumers within the state.[114] Both California and Massachusetts require companies collecting PII to implement a security policy in order to keep PII confidential.

Most states also have data-breach notification laws, which require businesses to notify consumers when their personal information has been compromised in a data breach.[115] The California Notice of Security Breach Act[116] requires any company that encounters a security breach of personal information of California citizens to notify those affected. Personal information includes names, addresses, driver's license numbers, and credit card information. California amended this law (which went into effect on January 1, 2012)[117] to require companies encountering a security breach affecting more than 500 California residents to notify the Attorney General of the breach, among other things.

California has also passed legislation which requires companies that collect PII to meet stringent security standards, such as those in the Payment Card Industry Data Security Standard (PCI DSS). PCI DSS is an information security standard for organizations that process debit and credit cards.[118] Minnesota also has a law based on PCI DSS.[119] The Minnesota law prohibits anyone conducting business in Minnesota from storing credit and debit card information. The law makes companies that do not comply with the PCI DSS liable for financial institutions' costs of canceling and replacing credit cards compromised in a security breach. Nevada specifically requires anyone doing business in Nevada that accepts credit card payments to comply with PCI DSS.[120]

4.6 WHAT HAPPENS IF I VIOLATE A COMPANY'S PRIVACY POLICY?

Besides being banned from using a website, you could be in violation of federal or state laws if you violate a website's privacy policy. The US Computer Fraud and Abuse Act[121] provides that anyone who "intentionally accesses a computer without authorization or exceeds authorized access, and thereby obtains information from any protected computer if the conduct involved an interstate or foreign communication shall be punished under the Act." Both criminal and civil actions may be brought under the act. In addition, if you are an employee of a company with a privacy policy and you violate that policy, you could be terminated.

4.7 WHAT HAPPENS IF I VIOLATE MY OWN PRIVACY POLICY?

This is a very serious matter. The FTC does bring actions against those who are found to have violated their own policies. Too often I see clients copying privacy policies from other websites thinking they are protected. Instead, they are subjecting themselves to more liability than if they had no policy at all.

First, the only state to currently require a privacy policy when a website collects information is California. If you are doing business there, you need to have this policy in place. Second, you must understand what information you collect and what you do with that information, and correctly explain that in your privacy policy.

The FTC recently entered into a settlement agreement with Epic Media Group, LLC, an online advertising company, which was using a tracking technology to discover the websites that consumers had visited in the past. Although its privacy policy indicated that it would only collect information about the consumers' visits to websites within its own advertising network, it actually collected information on consumers' visits to sites outside its network, "including sites relating to the users' personal health conditions and finances." The settlement agreement requires Epic to permanently delete and destroy all data collected in violation of the privacy policy.[122] This is an enormous waste of data collection that could have been avoided with a privacy policy that actually explained what Epic was doing and allowed users to opt out.

There have also been a number of high-profile actions by the FTC against major corporations regarding violations of their own privacy policies with respect to PII that they collect.[123] As a result of an FTC investigation involving Microsoft's Single Sign-in and Passport Wallet, Microsoft agreed to implement an information security program (which will be reviewed every two years) and to pay a fine of $10,000 for any future violations.

There have also been a number of recent actions by both the FTC and private individuals against social media companies for privacy violations. In the case of the Google Buzz social network,[124] the FTC found that Google led Gmail users to believe that they could choose whether or not they wanted to join the network. The problem was that the options for declining or leaving the social network did not work. According to the FTC, for users who expressly joined the Buzz social network, the instructions for the sharing of their personal information were confusing and difficult to find. The FTC also discovered that even those Gmail users who opted out were partially enrolled without their knowledge. In addition, Buzz shared with the public the identity of the individuals that the Gmail users most frequently emailed. Even those who elected to opt out after joining were not completely removed from Buzz.

Although the Buzz privacy policy stated: "When you sign up for a particular service that requires registration, we ask you to provide personal information. If we use this information in a manner different than the purpose for which it was collected, then we will ask for your consent prior to such use," Google did not in fact obtain consent.[125] Google settled with the FTC, agreeing to not make any further inaccurate privacy representations, to implement an effective privacy program, and to be subject to privacy audits for the next twenty years.

Similar FTC investigations against Twitter[126] and Facebook also resulted in settlements requiring the companies to make accurate privacy representations, obtain user consent prior to changing privacy settlings, institute an effective privacy program to protect users' information, and be subject to audits every two years for the next twenty years.[127]

What type of privacy policy you need depends on the industry you are in. However, if you collect any information from the users of your site, you really need to have an easily accessible and easy to understand written policy in place. This is discussed in more detail in Chapter 9. One of the complaints that other countries have about the United States is the lack of federal privacy regulations that apply generally to the Internet. The United States currently has federal regulations by industry, and each state has its own laws. Violations of these privacy regulations can result in civil and criminal penalties.

4.8 WHAT HAPPENS IF SOMEONE STEALS INFORMATION FROM MY WEBSITE?

The FTC will take action against businesses that experience a security breach when it appears that the business did not take "reasonable measures" to prevent the breach. Section 5 of the FTC Act prohibits "unfair or deceptive" trade practices, and that language has been used to authorize these FTC investigations. Most of these actions have resulted from the theft of credit card information from the businesses' sites. The FTC has taken the position that it is an unfair practice for a company to fail to follow its own privacy policy or, even if there is no privacy policy, fail to secure credit card information.

In the *Matter of BJ's Wholesale Club, Inc.* (FTC 2005),[128] the FTC began an investigation after there was a security breach at BJ's Wholesale Club that resulted in credit card information being compromised. Despite the fact that BJ's did not have a privacy policy in effect at the time, the FTC indicated that there were certain basic security measures that could have prevented the breach but had not been taken. As with most of these cases, BJ's settled with the FTC and agreed to implement an information security program to be reviewed every two years for the next twenty years.

There have also been some private lawsuits brought as a result of security breaches. It should be noted that the courts have consistently held that the plaintiff must show actual harm before bringing the suit. In other words, just because your information has been stolen does not mean you can sue. In *Resnick v. Avmed, Inc.*,[129] although the trial court dismissed the claims for negligence by the plaintiffs, indicating that injury could not be shown, the appellate court reversed the dismissal, holding that the identity theft that the plaintiffs suffered approximately one year after the theft was in fact sufficient injury to go ahead with the lawsuit. In *Resnick v. Avmed* two laptops containing the medical and financial information of 1.2 million consumers were stolen. The court said there was a sufficient relationship between the data which was stolen and the identity theft to show that damage had occurred as a result of the security breach.

In addition, a number of federal and state statutes allow private causes of action for security breaches. The Computer Fraud and Abuse Act specifically authorizes private causes of action by victims of identity theft.[130] States that permit private causes of action for security breaches include Alaska, California, Louisiana, Maryland, Massachusetts, Nevada, New Hampshire, North Carolina, Oregon, South Carolina, Tennessee, Virginia, and Washington.[131]

4.9 CAN I SEND COUPONS VIA TEXT MESSAGES?

Mobile spam is covered under two federal laws: the CAN-SPAM Act and the Telephone Consumer Protection Act (TCPA). The CAN-SPAM Act is designed to prevent false and misleading advertising, not necessarily any mobile advertising. Both the FTC (which enforces the CAN-SPAM Act) and the FCC (which enforces the TCPA) allow those bombarded with spam text messages to report the sender on their websites. The TCPA[132] institutes fines of $500 to $1,500 per violation regarding unsolicited text messages. A $250 million class action suit was recently filed against Papa John's for sending hundreds of thousands of unsolicited text messages to its customers through a mass texting service called OnTime4U.[133] Although the corporate headquarters told its franchisees to stop using OnTime4U to send out text messages, the corporation has been made party to the suit because it had originally recommended the marketing firm to its franchisees. What appears to have happened is that the franchisees gave their customers' phone numbers to the text marketing firm without getting the customers' consent in advance.

The FTC did bring an action under the CAN-SPAM Act in 2011 against Phillip A. Flora, who allegedly sent more than five million text messages over a forty-day period. The problem with cell phone spam, as opposed to email spam, is that some cell phone users have to pay for texts that they receive. When the recipients of the messages replied, Flora sold their information to marketers. Flora settled with the FTC by agreeing to pay a fine of $32,000 and stop sending spam text messages.[134]

As with email marketing, you should obtain advance written consent prior to sending out marketing text messages and adopt a method for the recipients to opt out. I imagine there will be new legislation soon regarding text message marketing.

4.10 DO I HAVE TO USE ENCRYPTED EMAIL?

It is never recommended that sensitive information be sent via email. Account numbers and social security numbers are especially at risk. There are also certain professions that need to be particularly careful with email communications, such as attorneys, doctors, and CPAs. Certain state bar associations, HIPAA, and the IRS do prohibit those covered from transmitting sensitive data via email. This means that you should be cautious about what you send in an email both for your protection and for the recipient's protection.

4.11 HOW FAR DO I HAVE TO GO TO KEEP CUSTOMER INFORMATION SECURE?

Personally identifiable information (PII) includes names, addresses, phone numbers, salaries, employers, and other information which can be used to identify a person and which may not be available publicly. As mentioned above, the United States has a patchwork of privacy laws that on a federal level apply to certain industries and on a state level to certain jurisdictions.

Recently, the federal government proposed that a "Consumer Privacy Bill of Rights" be enacted in order to safeguard consumer information placed on the Internet. It is meant to give individuals more control over how their personal information is used on the Internet and will consider requiring companies collecting information about individuals and their Internet activities to provide a "do not track" feature. While this is not yet a requirement, some companies have voluntarily enacted this technology on their websites.[135] To read the full report, go to:

www.whitehouse.gov/sites/default/files/privacy-final.pdf

The FTC has also come out with a report on its "best practices" for businesses that collect consumer data.[136] These practices include making privacy the default setting for consumers who submit their personal data online; providing a "do not track" feature on websites; and requiring data brokers to provide consumers access to the information that is being collected about them as well as the ability to correct errors. Because the FTC is the enforcing arm of privacy regulations, even though this report is suggestive, it is a good idea to follow through with its recommendations if you collect information from more than 5,000 users per year.[137]

There is no question that you must secure your clients' information. The FTC (as well as the agencies responsible for enforcing privacy laws) regularly investigates breaches of privacy policies, breaches of privacy laws, and data security breaches.[138]

There have been a number of private sector initiatives regarding privacy. While some are pushing for a national privacy statute, others feel better about self-monitoring in order to keep the government out of consumer privacy. The FTC noted such initiatives in its Commission's Privacy Report specifically mentioning "the Payment Card Institute Data Security Standards (PCI DSS) for payment card data, the SANS Institute's security policy templates, and standards and best practices guidelines for the financial services industry provided by BITS, the technology policy division of the Financial Services Roundtable."[139] Although the FTC Privacy Report suggested that other industries establish and implement best practices in data security, it also recommended that Congress pass data security and breach notification legislation.

The FTC also mentioned the settlements made with Google and Facebook and used those as an example of the minimum requirements of a privacy program for entities that collect information from consumers, including "(1) the designation of personnel responsible for the privacy program; (2) a risk assessment that, at a minimum, addresses employee training and management and product design and development; (3) the implementation of controls designed to address the risks identified; (4) appropriate oversight of service providers; and (5) evaluation and adjustment of the privacy program in light of regular testing and monitoring."[140] What this suggests is that also not yet codified, these procedures are what the FTC will be looking for when conducting an investigation. The FTC also encouraged encryption of consumer information by companies collecting such information.

In *United States v. RockYou Inc.*,[141] the social gaming site agreed to settle the charges against it that it failed to protect its 32 million users' email addresses and passwords. The FTC found that RockYou violated its own privacy policy, failed to secure user data, and violated the Children's Online Privacy Protection Act by collecting information on 179,000 users under the age of thirteen without verifiable parental consent. The settlement requires RockYou to pay a $250,000 fine, institute sufficient security measures to keep consumer data safe, delete all of the information it collected on children, and revise its data collection practices to comply with the law. It is important to note that the FTC explained this failure to keep the data secure as "not maintaining reasonable procedures, such as encryption to protect the confidentiality, security, and integrity of personal information collected from children." This seems to imply that encryption may be necessary in certain circumstances. The settlement also requires a review by an independent auditor of RockYou's security procedures every two years for the next twenty years.

Twitter has also been investigated by the FTC for failing to secure consumer information, which led to a data breach. In 2009 hackers gained access to Twitter accounts and generated unauthorized tweets from those accounts, including the accounts of President Obama and Fox News.[142] The hackers used password-guessing software to hack into the accounts and then changed the passwords, locking out the users. According to the FTC's complaint, "Twitter was vulnerable to these attacks because it failed to prevent unauthorized administrative control of its system, including reasonable steps to: require employees to use hard-to-guess administrative passwords that they did not use for other programs, websites, or networks; prohibit employees from storing administrative passwords in plain text within their personal e-mail accounts; suspend or disable administrative passwords after a reasonable number of unsuccessful login attempts; provide an administrative login web page that is made known only to authorized persons and is separate from the login page for users; enforce periodic changes of administrative passwords, for example, by setting them to expire every ninety days; restrict access to administrative controls to employees whose jobs required it; and impose other reasonable restrictions on administrative access, such as by restricting access to specified IP addresses."[143]

The settlement requires Twitter to increase its security measures to prevent unauthorized access to its accounts, revise its privacy and security policies to accurately describe what it does, and submit to an independent security audit every two years for the next ten years.

This is an especially big issue for those doing business overseas. The European Union currently has enormous concerns about the United States' lack of uniform federal privacy regulations. As such, the US Department of Commerce has had to develop a Safe Harbor privacy program. When a US company shows compliance with the Safe Harbor requirements, it can self-certify, which allows it to sell in the EU member states.

5 ····· EMPLOYMENT LAW ISSUES ······················

I n late 2010, the National Labor Relations Board (NLRB) brought an action against a company, American Medical Response (AMR), for firing an employee who made negative comments on her Facebook page about the company and her superior. Although the hearing was set for January 2011, the NLRB reported that they had settled with AMR who agreed to remove such provisions from its policies. The NLRB reported in a press release: "Under the terms of the settlement approved today by Hartford Regional Director Jonathan Kreisberg, the company agreed to revise its overly-broad rules to ensure that they do not improperly restrict employees from discussing their wages, hours and working conditions with co-workers and others while not at work, and that they would not discipline or discharge employees for engaging in such discussions."[144]

This is a very interesting case because, prior to this announcement, courts did permit companies to take adverse employment actions against employees who violated their company's social media policies. This case was different because the employee's comments were deemed by the NLRB to be related to her status as a union worker. In addition, the social media policy at issue was found to have violated labor laws by interfering with an employee's right to discuss working conditions with other employees. There have been a number of other actions instituted by the NLRB since then against employers regarding their social media policies and actions.[145]

In a rapidly developing subarea of Internet law, there has been an increasing number of lawsuits concerning actions taken by employers against employees for their online conduct, and by employees against employers for their conduct involving social media sites. While a company has the ability to monitor the activities of employees at work, it is unclear how far that right extends into an employee's activities while off duty. The limits are still being defined, but this chapter will give the reader some guidance as to what may and may not be actionable. It covers the circumstance in which adverse employment actions may be taken against an employee, the legal exceptions, the ability of an employer to monitor employee postings, the ability of a company to monitor employee emails, and a company's potential liability for an employee's online conduct. This chapter also discusses the rights of ownership of social media accounts after termination of employment and whether these rights lie with the employer or the former employee.

5.1 CAN EMPLOYEES BE FIRED FOR WHAT THEY POST ONLINE?

As discussed in the introduction, policies regarding the use of social media by employees must not violate the National Labor Relations Act,[146] which protects an employee's "right to . . . engage in . . . concerted activities for the purpose of . . . mutual aid or protection." In the *AMR* case,[147] the AMR employee made posts on Facebook after being denied union assistance in responding to an investigation. AMR then fired the employee for violating the company's social media policy by commenting about the situation on Facebook. AMR's policy expressly "barred employees from mentioning the company on Facebook or other social media sites." Another policy prohibited "disparaging . . . comments when discussing the company or the employee's superiors." According to the NLRB, those types of policies "constitute interference with employees in the exercise of their right to engage in protected concerted activity." Because the NLRB determined that the Facebook comments made by the employee were protected concerted activity under Section 7 of the National Labor Relations Act, it concluded that AMR's action in firing the employee and the company's social media policy were unlawful.

In another case involving the NLRB, the board allowed the firing of an employee for posts made on Facebook but held that the social media policy used by the company violated the National Labor Relations Act. In the case of *Knauz BMW*,[148] an employee was fired for posting photographs of a dealership car that had been driven into a pond with the caption: "This is your car. This is your car on drugs." The board indicated that, unlike in the case of *AMR*, this comment did not constitute "protected activity." The board did, however, find that "requiring courtesy" could infringe on an employee's right to engage in protected activity under the NLRA. Because of this, the board ruled that the policy violated the act. The offending provision read, "No one should be disrespectful or use profanity or other language which injures the image or reputation of the Dealership." The board concluded that this provision seemed to discourage employees' protected rights to discuss the terms and conditions of their employment. What is important about this case is that employers do have the ability to fire employees for what they post on Facebook *except* if what they post is protected under Section 7 of the NLRA.[149]

The takeaway from these two cases is: (1) Section 7 protections apply to both union and nonunion employees alike[150] (although the employee in AMR was a union member, the car salesman in Knauz was not), and (2) employers cannot ban negative comments made by their employees about the workplace on social media sites when they consist of protected concerted activity. The NLRB compares posts on Facebook to discussions "around the water cooler."[151] While employers do not have to allow defamatory or discriminatory comments or permit an employee to breach confidentiality requirements or engage in product disparagement, they do need to tolerate workplace grumblings, which are protected.[152] In any event, in an employment at will state, employers can fire anyone for any reason as long as the reason does not violate the law. See question 5.8 (What state laws apply to employer actions regarding an employee's online activities?).

5.2 CAN AN EMPLOYER USE SUBTERFUGE TO EXAMINE A FUTURE EMPLOYEE'S OR CURRENT EMPLOYEE'S ONLINE PROFILE?

No. There are both federal and state laws that make this practice illegal. Maryland was the first to pass a law prohibiting employers from requesting or requiring passwords to social media sites;[153] California, Delaware, Illinois, Michigan, and New Jersey also passed similar laws, and legislation is pending in fourteen other states.[154] Michigan's law,[155] for example, makes it a misdemeanor for an employer to: "(a) Request an employee or an applicant for employment to grant access to, allow observation of, or disclose information that allows access to or observation of the employee's or applicant's personal internet account. (b) Discharge, discipline, fail to hire, or otherwise penalize an employee or applicant for employment for failure to grant access to, allow observation of, or disclose information that allows access to or observation of the employee's or applicant's personal internet account."

At the federal level, this type of conduct has been found to violate the Stored Communications Act (SCA). The SCA prohibits the intentional accessing of electronic information without authorization. In *Pietrylo v. Hillstone Restaurant Group*,[156] two employees created a password-protected

Myspace page for the use of employees wanting to vent about their employer. When the managers learned of the page, they obtained the password from one of the employees who had access to the page. The creators of the page were fired and brought suit alleging, among other things, that the managers had violated the SCA. Because the jury found that the employee felt pressured to give the managers the password, the court was able to conclude that the mangers had accessed the site without authorization and held them liable for violating the SCA. It is also possible that reviewing an employee's online profile prior to hiring him or her could violate the Fair Credit Reporting Act (FCRA),[157] which indicates what information can be accessed and how such information can be used with respect to background checks of prospective employees.

In a Facebook post[158] by Erin Egan, Facebook's Chief Privacy Officer, Facebook has expressly warned employers not to ask applicants for their passwords. The post went so far as to say: "Facebook takes your privacy seriously. We'll take action to protect the privacy and security of our users, whether by engaging policymakers or, where appropriate, by initiating legal action, including by shutting down applications that abuse their privileges."

What this means is that employers should not be asking potential or current employees to provide social media site passwords. In question 5.7, ownership of social media accounts opened by employees but used for company purposes will be discussed. In addition, examining a prospective employee's Facebook page could reveal information about the candidate, such as race and religion, that the employer would be better off not knowing. Such access and failure to hire such a candidate could lead to a discrimination suit.

5.3 TO WHAT EXTENT CAN A BUSINESS MONITOR AN EMPLOYEE'S USE OF THE INTERNET AT WORK?

Although it would be an invasion of your privacy if I read all of your personal emails without your permission, employers have been doing this since email became popular. It is generally accepted that content placed on a company-owned computer or sent through the company email system can be reviewed by the company.[159] The reason behind this is not just to make sure you are doing your work but also to protect the employer from discrimination and harassment lawsuits. Whether or not the employer should monitor emails and whether they can monitor personal emails sent with an employee's password-protected account is another issue. Most of the lawsuits by employees for invasion of privacy against their employers come down to whether or not the employee was told in advance of the employer's monitoring practice.

This area of law is covered by both federal and state statutes, as well as common law. Under the Electronic Communications Privacy Act (ECPA)[160] companies are permitted to monitor employees' emails when: the employee has consented (through signing an employee handbook acknowledgement or other written policy); there is a legitimate business reason; or the company monitors emails to comply with its own antiharassment or discrimination policies. Although federal law does not require that the employees be notified of an employer's monitoring activities, some state laws do.[161] Notifying an employee of the monitoring will help the employer if sued for invasion of privacy.

Because of the liability of companies for failing to stop sexual harassment or discrimination, or creating a hostile work environment, it could be argued that companies have a duty to monitor employee email messages and Internet usage at work. Offensive emails and websites cause employees to feel harassed and can contribute to a hostile work environment. There is also the possibility of racially offensive jokes being circulated by email. A company can have a policy prohibiting these things, but if the company is not monitoring it, how can it know whether or not employees comply with the policy?

In *Vandell v. Chevron Corporation*,[162] Chevron had to pay $2.2 million to settle a sexual harassment case brought by four female employees who said "they had been the targets of a barrage of offensive jokes, E-mail messages and comments about their clothes and body parts, and, in one case, sadistic pornography sent through the company mail."[163] It was clear that the corporation did nothing to monitor the employees' Internet conduct, which created the conditions of which the women complained.

If you are an employer, it is a good idea to create an email/Internet usage policy that lets employees know that their online activities may be monitored at work. The policy should be signed by each employee and specifically state that employees should have no expectation of privacy with respect to anything they do on their work computer or work cell phone. The policy should also expressly prohibit discriminatory or harassing emails and prohibit accessing pornography or other offensive sites from a work computer or phone. Finally, employees should be warned that violation of the policy could result in disciplinary action, up to and including termination.

5.4 TO WHAT EXTENT CAN A BUSINESS MONITOR AN EMPLOYEE'S USE OF THE INTERNET OUTSIDE OF WORK?

It depends on the policies your employer has in place and the laws of the state in which you reside. There are a number of issues regarding what an employee does at home. First, it is unlawful in some states to take an adverse employment action for something entirely legal that an employee does on his or her own time. Second, if by monitoring an employee's use of the Internet outside of work means spying on the employee's social media sites, we would need to determine if the employer is looking at things that have been posted by the employee for public viewing or not. Third, it will also depend on whether the nature of the outside Internet usage involves the company, its employees, or its products.

In some states legal off-hours conduct is protected to varying degrees. Off-hours use of social media would most likely be protected in California, Colorado, New York, and North Dakota, where the statutes provide protection for employees who engage in lawful activities outside the workplace.[164] In other states the language is more specific; for example, Minnesota law[165] indicates: "An employer may not refuse to hire a job applicant or discipline or discharge an employee because the applicant or employee engages in or has engaged in the use or enjoyment of lawful consumable products, if the use or enjoyment takes place off the premises of the employer during nonworking hours. For purposes of this section, 'lawful consumable products' means products whose use or enjoyment is lawful and which are consumed during use or enjoyment, and includes food, alcoholic or nonalcoholic beverages, and tobacco."

Although these laws are intended to protect alcohol and tobacco use outside the workplace, it is possible that these laws could one day be extended to include social media use. There are laws like these in twenty-nine states.[166]

The second issue is whether the employer is viewing the employees' social media posts (Facebook, Twitter, etc.) with permission or with public posts. If employees are making posts that can be viewed by the public, the employer would not be invading their privacy. If the employer obtained an employee's password in order to monitor his or her online activity, this is an entirely different issue. All fifty states and the federal government have laws making this conduct illegal.[167]

Finally, if the employee makes posts about the company or its products, because of the potential for liability for the company, the company has an interest in monitoring such posts. See question 5.5 regarding vicarious liability.

5.5 CAN A COMPANY BE VICARIOUSLY LIABLE FOR THE POSTS OF AN EMPLOYEE?

Vicarious liability exists when one entity can be held liable for the acts of another. When an employer is held liable for the acts of its employee, it is called respondeat superior. Liability attaches to the employer when the employee is acting within the scope of his employment.[168] It does not matter whether or not the employer is aware of the conduct giving rise to liability.

Under this theory, employee posts may subject the company to liability. If an employee makes false statement about its company's products or the products of its competitor, the company could be subject to an FTC action for false advertising under the Lanham Act or the FTC Endorsement Guides. The biggest risk is for fake reviews. A company should not only not direct employees or independent contractors to post fake reviews but should also seek to educate anyone using social media on its behalf to not post reviews unless they are truthful and reveal a person's relationship with the company.

As discussed in Chapter 3, the FTC Endorsement Guides indicate that the relationship between the poster and the company must be disclosed. In other words, if an employee is making favorable posts about a company's product and fails to disclose that he works for the company, the company may be held liable. Even if the post is completely truthful, the failure to disclose the relationship can create liability for the company. Again, companies need to inform their employees and independent contractors of these risks to avoid these types of actions.

5.6 CAN A COMPANY FORCE THE REMOVAL OF INFORMATION FROM A THIRD-PARTY SITE WHEN SUCH INFORMATION WAS POSTED BY AN EMPLOYEE?

Because of the potential for vicarious liability for employers with respect to posts made by employees, the company must take action to force the removal of any violating posts. These would include defamatory or discriminatory comments about other employees, breaches of confidentiality, or product disparagement, as well as any posts violating the FTC Endorsement Guides. Although these types of cases are very fact dependent, it would be helpful for companies to have Internet usage and social media policies that address these issues.

It should be noted that there are, however, federal and state laws that could prevent an employer from taking adverse action based upon an employee's off-duty social media conduct. These laws include the National Labor Relations Act, state laws that prohibit adverse action based on an employee's lawful off-duty activities, discrimination laws, and whistle-blower protection laws. Although an employer may be able to request that an employee remove offending material, if the employee refused, the employer may be justified in terminating such employee.

All companies have to monitor their trademarks or risk losing them. By conducting social media searches, companies can discover potential infringement or other violations of law. Whether or not the person making the offending post is an employee, the company does have recourse under the Digital Millennium Copyright Act (DMCA), which permits the owner of the intellectual property to request that the offending post be removed. In addition, Facebook and other social media sites have terms of use that also address these issues. Thus, the company can contact the site where the offending material exists and submit what is known as a takedown notice. While the DMCA applies specifically to copyrights, the terms of use of these social media sites appear to apply to all intellectual property rights, including trademarks.

Getting defamatory material removed from a social media site is a bit more difficult than getting infringing material removed. The Communications Decency Act (CDA) protects websites or other Internet service providers from liability for offending content posted by third parties. This means that there is no requirement that they remove offending material, even if they have received notice of it (this could change in the future). From a practical perspective, you would want to first contact the poster of the offending material and ask this person to remove it. If he or she is your employee or independent contractor and the post clearly violates his or her agreement or your policy and is not otherwise protected, you may terminate this person. However, this does not remove the offending material from the Internet. Your second step would be to send a takedown notice to the website and see what happens. Again, the site owners are not obligated to remove it, but if it does violate their terms of use, they may. If this does not work, you may need to hire an attorney to send a cease-and-desist letter to the poster of the comment.

This is not without risk, however, because such cases seem to reflect poorly on those seeking to have offending material removed. The people who post defamatory comments in the first place are more likely to also post copies of any demands to take it down. Sometimes it looks like the offended party is trying to squelch free speech or is overly sensitive. With the case of *North Face v. South Butt*, the offending material got much more exposure after it was complained about by North Face. Regardless, if the comment is not about your company but about a competitor and you could be vicariously liable, you should try to have it removed as soon as possible.

5.7 WHAT RECOURSE DO EMPLOYEES HAVE AGAINST AN EMPLOYER WHO TRIES TO TAKE OWNERSHIP OF THEIR SOCIAL MEDIA ACCOUNTS?

There are a number of pending lawsuits regarding this very issue. It appears that whether or not there is a written agreement between the employer and employee regarding the ownership of the accounts may be important. In addition, there can be liability for a company to take control of employees' social media accounts without their consent. The issue may come down to whether or not Twitter followers or Facebook friends constitute a protected client list.

In *Maremont v. Susan Fredman Design Group, Ltd.*,[169] the court allowed claims that an employer was found liable for accessing an employee's social media accounts without the employee's authorization under both the Stored Communications Act and the Lanham Act to proceed. While Maremont, the Director of Marketing for Susan Fredman Design, was in the hospital, the design firm accessed her accounts and made posts and tweets as though they were from Maremont. The court indicated that to succeed on her claims, she must be able to show damages.

In *PhoneDog v. Kravitz*,[170] both the employer and employee are claiming ownership of a Twitter account used to promote the employer's services. The employee kept the account and changed the password to prevent the employer from accessing it. The court has denied the motion to dismiss and is allowing this claim to proceed to trial. In *Ardis Health, LLC v. Nankivell*,[171] the court ordered a former employee to turn over the passwords to the plaintiff's social media accounts, clearly taking the position that they were owned by the employer. It is of note that in this case the employer had a written social media policy, whereas the employer in the *PhoneDog* case did not.

Your best protection here is to (1) have a policy regarding the ownership of these accounts and (2) have your company register these accounts in its own name as administrator so they cannot be locked out by a former employee. This can also be a strategy for reducing the chances of trademark infringement as discussed in Chapter 2. Registering your trademarks on Twitter, Facebook, etc. and reserving the domain names will help prevent others from co-opting your intellectual property.

5.8 WHAT STATE LAWS APPLY TO EMPLOYER ACTIONS REGARDING AN EMPLOYEE'S ONLINE ACTIVITIES?

In this chapter we have reviewed some of the federal laws that govern an employer's actions with respect to an employee's online activities. There is the National Labor Relations Act,[172] which protects employees from adverse employment actions when engaging in protected activities (which include discussing working conditions online). This type of claim has been asserted against employers who have fired employees for their Facebook posts. The Stored Communications Act[173] prohibits the intentional accessing of electronic information without authorization. This type of claim has been asserted when employers have accessed employee social media accounts without authorization. The Electronic Communications Privacy Act[174] prohibits the intentional interception of electronic communications. This type of claim has been used in cases involving an employer's reading of employees' emails. The Lanham Act[175] Section 43(a) prohibits false endorsements, which occur "when a person's identity is connected with a product or service in such a way that consumers are likely to be misled about that person's sponsorship or approval of the product or service."[176] This type of claim has been asserted against employers who make posts using an employee's social media account without that person's consent. We also discussed the potential for a company's liability under the FTC Endorsement Guides for posts made by an employee. In addition, the Fair Credit Reporting Act[177] includes rules regarding the background checks of prospective employees, which may be applied to social media checks (but have not yet been).

There are a number of state laws regarding employment relationships, and they vary significantly from state to state. Common law is law created by court cases.[178] While these types of lawsuits are not based on a statute, they can be brought if the court in that jurisdiction recognizes such cause of action. These causes of action could include defamation, invasion of privacy, and intentional infliction of emotional distress.

In addition, some states are at-will employment states, and others have significant carve-outs that put conditions on an employer's ability to terminate an employee. Regardless, if the reason for terminating an employee is unlawful, there could be a lawsuit. Wrongful discharge includes firing someone for a discriminatory reason, for performing a public duty (like jury duty), whistle blowing, retaliation, refusal to commit an illegal act, or when a company fails to follow its own termination procedures or fires someone in violation of his or her employment contract. It is also clear that firing someone who is exercising their rights under the National Labor Relations Act is prohibited, as we have seen with some recent cases.

There are many state statutes that govern these relationships as well. Most states have privacy laws that govern to what extent an employer can monitor an employee's computer usage. States also have pre-employment inquiry statutes that may prohibit requiring an employee to provide their social media account passwords. As discussed in question 5.2, a number of states have recently enacted statutes (and a large number have legislation pending) that prohibit employers from requesting, and in some cases viewing, an employee's social media accounts. As discussed in question 5.4, there are state laws that protect an employee's right to engage in legal conduct during his or her off-hours.

What this means is that if you are fired for your online conduct and you believe your conduct was lawful or that the firing is a pretext for discriminatory treatment, you would be well served to at least run the circumstances by an employment law attorney. This is a rapidly changing area of law, and I expect there to be a slew of new state laws regarding such types of situations over the next couple of years.

5.9 SHOULD A BUSINESS HAVE A WRITTEN INTERNET USAGE POLICY?

There are a number of issues which a company needs to address regarding an employee's work computer and work phone usage, Internet usage, social media usage, and any communication regarding the company or its products that could be considered confidential. The problem, of course, is that the law is changing so rapidly that what may be in your policy today may violate the law tomorrow.

Regardless, there are some issues that should be addressed. First, you should not permit employees to use mobile devices to store confidential company information. There is a risk not only of loss of the device but also that the information will be available to the employee after he or she leaves the company. This is obviously a difficult issue when so many people use their phones and tablets for work purposes. You should revise any employment agreements to address these confidentially issues, including the ownership of social media accounts, names, and content. Failure to address this issue can result in a company's losing a Twitter handle or Facebook page due to an employee's claim of ownership. If you have a strong agreement in place regarding the protection of your intellectual property, you will avoid some of the issues employers are now facing.

Second, your employee handbook should be updated to include all electronic communications, website viewing, and online posting as potential conduct that could give rise to disciplinary action for harassment or discrimination. Cyberbullying should also be explained and prohibited. Revealing confidential information or trade secrets over the Internet should be expressly prohibited. With respect to the use of social media, because the NLRB has found companies to be in violation of the NLRA for taking adverse action against employees who post comments on social media sites regarding working condition, it is not a good idea to prohibit social media posts. You should prohibit posts that are discriminatory or harassing, violate the FTC Endorsement Guides, disparage a competitors' business or product, or breach the company's confidentiality policies and agreements or federal or state privacy statutes.

It is also important to educate your employees on the damage social media posts can have on both the company and the employee. There are not only privacy, intellectual property, and advertising laws that they need to be aware of, but also the potential for criminal charges due to their online conduct. A company has a vested interest in protecting its trade secrets and goodwill. Because employees now have a way to reach millions of readers in a very short amount of time, it is imperative that the company be proactive in order to prevent litigation with both its employees and its competitors. These policies should also be communicated to independent contractors, especially with respect to endorsements.

5.10 DON'T EMPLOYEES HAVE A FIRST AMENDMENT RIGHT OF FREE SPEECH?

While employees do have a right of free speech, they must also remember that their right does not prevent them from being fired. Most states are at-will employment states and permit an employer to fire anyone at any time without cause, unless there is a cause that violates the law (discrimination, for example). Although social media posts would be considered free speech, unless the post is protected under the National Labor Relations Act or some other federal or state law, an employee can be fired for making them.

While you do have a right of free speech, it can be restricted in the workplace for a variety of legal reasons. You need to be aware of the company's policy regarding social media as well as any other restriction on speech in the workplace. For example, public employees are significantly limited in their political speech in the workplace. But as mentioned earlier, employees in states that prohibit adverse employment actions for legal off-duty conduct may be better protected for their social media posts.

6 PROTECTING YOUR NAME
AND THE WORK YOU CREATE

In the 2008 Texas case of *Healix Infusion Therapy, Inc. v. Murphy*,[179] the business that owned the registered trademark HEALIX for its in-home infusion therapy system sued a competitor, Dr. Murphy, for registering the domain names "Helixhealth.org" and "Myhelixhealth.com/.org." Note the difference in spelling between "Healix," the infusion therapy company, and "Helix," the health services company. The Texas court granted Murphy's motion for summary judgment on Healix's cybersquatting claim, essentially permitting Murphy to continue to use the domain names, which were very similar to Healix's trademark.

How could this have happened? Isn't it cybersquatting when someone registers a domain name confusingly similar to an actual trademark? Not so fast: Intellectual property law is not so clear-cut. There are a number of nuances and exceptions to almost every rule. In the *Healix* case, the court sided with Murphy because Healix was unable to show bad faith on the part of Murphy (which is required under the Anticybersquatting Act). Not only are you required to follow legal protocol when registering a trademark, but in order to keep it, you must also properly enforce it. This chapter will discuss how to protect your name, your content, and the rest of the work that you have created.

Intellectual property is the bread and butter of most online businesses. It is governed by different rules than personal property and real property. In order to protect the work you create, you have to follow the law. Failure to do so will result in the loss of your intellectual property. Intellectual property includes your business name, your blog's name, the names of your products and services, your photographs, logos, drawings, written content, graphic images, and much more. Some of these items are protected by trademark law and others by copyright law. This chapter will discuss how to protect the name of your online presence and the work that you create. It explains the differences between trademarks, copyrights, trade secrets, and patents, which are the four main types of intellectual property. It describes how to protect these types of intellectual property from infringement and cybersquatting when your rights are created. It also addresses the issues involved in registering your intellectual property with state and federal agencies.

6.1 WHAT IS INTELLECTUAL PROPERTY?

When you think of property, you think of things you own, like your car or your house. Your car is considered personal property because it is movable. Your house is considered real property because it is attached to the land. The third type of property you may own is your intellectual property. Intellectual property rights attach to the things you create. They include the name under which you do business, the articles you write, the videos you shoot, and the doodles you draw. Intellectual property can be divided into the categories of trademarks, copyrights, trade secrets, and patents. Although some of your creations may fit under more than one category of intellectual property, the laws governing them are very different. Generally, anything you create is your property, but intellectual property law helps you keep your economic advantage by preventing others from using your work or negatively affecting the goodwill associated with your name or business.

After you have gone through all of the effort to set up your online presence, you will want to protect it from imitators and detractors. Most importantly, you will want to make sure that no one else uses your trade name. Your trade name is the name with which you want people to associate your business or online presence.

6.2 WHAT IS A TRADEMARK OR SERVICE MARK?

A trademark or service mark is "a word, phrase, symbol or design, or a combination of words, phrases, symbols or designs, that identifies and distinguishes the source of the goods or services of one party from those of others."[180] A trademark applies to goods, and a service mark applies to services. For ease of explaining, I will use the terms "trademark" and "mark" to refer to both a trademark and a service mark, respectively. Trademarks can include logos, colors, images, and abbreviations. Trademark rights attach as soon as a trademark is used in commerce in association with a good or service. If you were to sell teddy bears under the name Kelly's Teddies, you would have trademark rights in that name and could prevent others from selling teddy bears under the brand name Kelly's Teddies even if you have not registered the trademark with the US Patent and Trademark Office (USPTO).

In addition to this common-law trademark right, there are state laws that allow you to register your mark.[181] Typically, state trademark registration only applies to the state's jurisdiction within that particular state but does provide more protection than the common-law rights described above. In any event, a prior federal trademark registration preempts both common-law and state-law trademark protection. If you have significant dollars invested in your mark, it would probably be better for you to register your mark federally because of the additional protection that registration would afford you.

6.3 WHAT IS FEDERAL TRADEMARK PROTECTION?

In addition to common-law protection and state registration, you also have the option to register your trademark with the USPTO. Federal trademark registration provides several benefits over common-law and state protection, including triple damages and attorney fees for willful infringement. Federal registration also "provides notice to the public of the registrant's claim of ownership of the mark, a legal presumption of ownership nationwide, and the exclusive right to use the mark on or in connection with the goods or services set forth in the registration."[182] Trademark registrations initially last ten years and must be renewed every ten years. In order to keep your trademark protection, you must constantly monitor your mark and prevent others from using it by sending cease-and-desist letters as well as taking infringers to court to enjoin them from using your mark.[183]

In order to register your mark, you must meet the Lanham Act's[184] requirements. This is the federal statute governing trademarks. The law is pretty complex, but the following is an explanation of what terms can be trademarked. The statute permits registration for names that are distinctive and associated with your product or service. When a name is deemed "generic" or "merely descriptive," it is not eligible for trademark law protection. You will probably not be able to register the name Life Coach for your coaching business, as it would most likely be deemed generic. If you have a coaching service directed at teens, you may not be able to register the name Teen's Coaching Service because you would merely be describing the service. Inspiroteen is stronger than a descriptive name because it suggests rather than describes the service you are providing (inspiring teens). If you had numerous coaches working under you, you could go with something like Wimberley Enterprises [185] because the recognized meaning is not associated with your product or service and would be considered arbitrary. In the alternative, you could try Flizzle, a fanciful made-up word with no independent meaning. Words that are suggestive, arbitrary, and fanciful can be registered. Because the USPTO attorneys often reject applications for reasons that are incomprehensible to anyone other than trademark attorneys, and sometimes even to them, you may want to consider consulting an intellectual property attorney when seeking to register a mark.

6.4 HOW DO I PROTECT MY MARK?

Even if you are not selling products or services but merely providing information through online publishing or blogging, you may want to use trademarks to identify your work to the public and protect your brand. [186] In order to show that you intend to claim protection under trademark law, you could put a ™ or SM (depending on whether it is a trademark [™] or service mark [SM]) immediately after the name or other identifying material that you would like to protect. The ™ or SM symbol will put people on notice that you are claiming trademark rights, but it is not required to protect your mark. You can put a ® after your mark only if you have actually registered it with the USPTO.

The idea behind trademark law is to prevent confusion in the marketplace about the source of goods and services. It also is designed to protect the owner of a trademark from others co-opting it for financial gain. As mentioned above, once a name is put into commerce, you can claim common-law trademark protections, but you can also register it at the state and federal levels for increased levels of protection.

If you have obtained a domain name that matches the name you use to identify your online presence, you should consider registering similar domain names with as many different extensions as possible. This will prevent others from trying to divert traffic from your blog to theirs by confusing people searching for your site. For example, if your blog is known as Belinda's Blog, you can register Belindasblog.com, Belindasblog.net, Belindasblog.biz, Belindasblog.org, etc. If you own these domain names, people who may try to co-opt your readership will be unable to obtain these alternate names.

If somebody does register your trade name with a different domain name ending, it is possible that liability could result if you can show that this registration was made in bad faith. In other words, if the business who registered the second domain name did so to capitalize on the success of the original site, that would tend to show bad faith. Because the domain name registrar does not check for trademark infringement, it is possible for someone to register a domain name that is actually someone else's trade name. This does not mean that it is automatically prohibited (again, only bad faith registration is prohibited). Another step that you will need to take to protect your trademark is to occasionally run your name though a search engine to locate potential infringement. If you find others using your mark, you will need to determine whether their use is a permitted use.[187] If it is not, you will need to take action to stop their use or risk losing your rights to the mark. Enforcing your intellectual property rights is discussed in Chapter 7.

6.5 HOW DO I REGISTER MY TRADEMARK?

Although you can do it yourself, the registration process is very complicated. The attorneys who work for the USPTO usually reject the applications, even when filed by an attorney. Their comments are often difficult to decipher, so it is hard to correct the errors they point out. If you do decide to register your trademark or service mark with the USPTO on your own, you can fill out their application online at www.uspto.gov. You will first need to make sure that the name you are choosing can be registered and is available. How to choose a name was discussed in question 6.3. There is a database on the USPTO website that you can access to check for previously registered names. The USPTO database is known as the Trademark Electronic Search System database. This database contains all of the registered names at the USPTO. You will want to make sure that your name is (1) sufficiently unique, (2) different enough from the previously registered names, and (3) not already registered or otherwise in use.[188]

The fee to register online is $275 or $325 depending on the class of goods and services indicated (compared to $375 per class of goods and services if filed by mail). In addition to the identity of the class of goods or services, which you can search for on the USPTO website, you will need the date of the mark's first use in commerce and a copy of the design component to the mark you are seeking, if any. If your desired trademark is also your domain name, it is best to leave off the .com extension.

Generally, you will receive a written response to your application within six months of filing, according to the USPTO website. Please note that you will not get your application fee back if the USPTO does not register your mark. Not only is it a good idea to use an intellectual property attorney for filing the application, but it is also a good idea to use one to help determine if your name can even be registered.

6.6 WHAT IS TRADEMARK INFRINGEMENT?

Trademark infringement occurs when someone uses your mark without your consent in a way that is likely to confuse the public about the source of the product or service being offered. If someone starts providing coaching services under the name Wimberley Enterprises when you have been using that name for a number of years, that person would be committing trademark infringement whether or not you have a federally registered trademark. If a person started using Wimberley Enterprises for his or her local real estate business, he or she would probably not be deemed to be infringing on your mark as it is not likely consumers would be confused as to the source of the service (i.e., they would not use the real estate company believing they were relying on the reputation of your coaching service).[189]

In one recent case a federal court ruled that the University of South Carolina could not register its "SC" trademark because it was likely to be confused with the University of Southern California's "SC" registered trademark, which had already been registered.[190] The lesson here is that if you plan on using a mark on a national basis, it is better to be the first to register it.

When someone commits trademark infringement, there are two possible remedies. First, an injunction to stop the infringement can be issued by a court. An injunction is an order to stop someone from doing something. Second, the infringer may become liable for damages to the trademark owner. Statutory damages include the infringer's profit from the use of the owner's mark, any damages incurred by the owner, and the owner's attorney fees in bringing the infringement action. In order to establish trademark infringement, you must first establish that (1) you own the mark, (2) someone else used the mark, (3) the use was in connection with the sale or advertising of goods and services, and (4) the use was without your consent.[191]

There are a number of defenses to trademark infringement that may be asserted. First, as in the example given above regarding the Wimberley Enterprises, there is little likelihood of confusion between the original use and the alleged infringing use. Second, fair use defenses apply here as well. If the alleged infringing use is for a news report, parody, educational purpose, or criticism, it will probably be held an acceptable use. Third, if the trademark owner fails to take prompt action against the alleged infringer, the owner could lose on the basis of laches. Laches means that the owner unreasonably delayed enforcing his or her trademark rights and that the infringer was in some way prejudiced by the delay.[192]

6.7 WHAT IS CYBERSQUATTING?

Cybersquatting occurs when someone sells, purchases, registers, licenses, or otherwise uses a domain name with a "bad faith" intent to profit from someone else's trademark. Congress passed the Anticybersquatting Consumer Protection Act in 1999[193] to stop people from purchasing domain names for the sole purpose of selling them to the owners of the associated trademarks. In determining whether bad faith is present, a court will consider whether the purchaser intended to divert customers from a legitimate owner's online location, whether the new site could harm the mark's goodwill, and if the owner of the domain name tried to sell the domain name to the trademark owner without having used it first. Damages are significant under this act. You should note that just because someone has your mark in his or her domain name does not mean that there was bad faith on that person's part. There is another mechanism to challenge a domain name through the Internet Corporation for Assigned Names and Numbers (ICANN) registrar.

Let's say you register the business name Flizzle for trademark protection with the USPTO. You have also purchased the domain name Flizzle.com for a website where you link consumers with life, health, and business coaches in their geographic areas. If after you become successful someone else purchases a group of the Flizzle domain names with alternative endings (such as .biz and .net) and starts providing the same service on these sites, cybersquatting would appear to have occurred. You can bring a claim either under the Anticybersqatting Consumer Protection Act or through the ICANN process.[194] You might also have a trademark infringement claim. All of these options are discussed more fully in Chapter 7.

6.8 WHAT IS A COPYRIGHT?

A copyright is a type of intellectual property. Copyright law protects "original works of authorship."[195] If you create an original piece of work, you get to control its use and distribution. Examples of works that may be copyrightable include blog posts, articles, books, photographs, drawings, images, videos, podcasts, musical works, and software. The work must be original, creative, and fixed in a tangible form (not just an idea in your mind). You have copyright law protection as soon as you fix your work in permanent form. When a blogger types a blog post, a photographer takes a photograph, or a student shoots a video, copyright protection is created. In addition, posting something directly on the Internet is fixing it in permanent form. Copyright law protects all of these works, regardless of whether they have been registered with the US Copyright Office or not.

You will own the copyright in a work if you created it or if it was created by your employee. Otherwise, you will need a written agreement with the creator of the work transferring the ownership rights to you. A license agreement will grant you the right to use someone else's work usually for a limited time or purpose. While some bloggers believe that they also own comments made to their blogs, this is not true. Unless you have an agreement transferring the ownership of comments to you, the people who posted the comments will own the copyright to them. This means that you would not be able to copy or repost their comments anyplace else. The way to address this issue is by adopting terms of use that grant you either ownership or a license to use their comments. This issue is discussed more thoroughly in Chapter 9.

Copyright infringement is a serious concern for those who post content on the Internet. You will want to prevent others from copying or modifying your work without your consent. Copyright enforcement is discussed in Chapter 7. Similar to trademark law, however, others may use your work without your permission for "fair use" purposes.

6.9 WHAT DOES A COPYRIGHT PROTECT?

Copyright law protects the "expression" of ideas. You are the copyright owner of the actual wording of a blog you composed and posted, not the subject matter in general. Copyright law does not protect single words, phrases, titles, ideas, procedures, systems, methods of operation, databases, or facts; content that is in the public domain; content for which the copyright has expired; and content authored by the US government. For example, the title of your blog post cannot by itself be copyright protected. As mentioned earlier, there is also an exception to copyright protection for "fair uses"[196] such as reporting, commentary, criticism, parody, and teaching. Since 1990, "moral rights" to works are also protected. Moral rights prevent later owners from destroying or altering copyrighted works. Public facts cannot be copyrighted (such as publicly available names and phone numbers).

Copyright ownership grants you the exclusive right to control the use and distribution of your copyrighted work. This means you can decide who can copy your blog post (unless the copy is fair use). Your rights include the exclusive ability to make copies of the work, create derivative works, sell copies of the work, license the work, and publicly display or perform the work.[197] As the owner of the copyright, you can either sell your work outright or license it. Licensing means that you keep ownership of your copyright but are allowing someone to use your work for a limited time and purpose, usually in exchange for payment. If someone uses your work without your permission or contrary to a license agreement, you may bring a claim against such person or entity in court. Although your original work is automatically protected from the moment the work is created in fixed form, there are two additional steps you can take: You can place a copyright notice on your work and register your work with the US Copyright Office.

6.10 HOW LONG DOES COPYRIGHT REGISTRATION LAST?

If you register your work with the US Copyright Office, protection generally lasts for seventy years after the death of the original author if the author is an individual.[198] It will last ninety-five years from the date of publication or 120 years from the date of creation in the case of unpublished works if the author is a company. Although a company owns the copyright in all works created by its employees in the normal course of business, it must have a written agreement to transfer ownership to it from any independent contractors.

It should be noted that failure to obtain a written agreement giving you ownership of the intellectual property that the independent contractor creates on your behalf could result in the independent contractor owning it. I have seen this happen with photographers and website designers. Oral agreements are not enforceable. Make sure you spell out the ownership of any work created by nonemployees or obtain a document transferring ownership to you before you pay for the work.

6.11 WHAT IS A COPYRIGHT NOTICE?

A copyright notice is your claim of copyright in your work. It generally includes the word "copyright" or the copyright symbol ©, the year of first

publication, and the name of the owner of the copyright: for example, ©
2013 Kimberly A. Houser. You should note that most countries outside of
the United States will not recognize the word "copyright" but only the symbol
©. By displaying a copyright notice on your work, you are putting the public
on notice that you are asserting copyright ownership of the work and that
your work is protected by copyright law. You do not need to register your
work with the US Copyright Office before putting the notice on it. The © is
similar to the ™ and ᴿᴹ in trademark law. These symbols are not required to
make a claim of infringement. They can be used even if your copyright or
trademark is not registered. This notice will defeat a claim that someone was
unaware of your copyright ownership.

6.12 SHOULD I REGISTER MY COPYRIGHT?

Although you do not need to register your work in order to protect it, registration with the US Copyright Office provides the following advantages:

- It is a public record and notice to the world of your copyright claim
  in your work.
- You have the ability to bring a claim in a US court (even if you do not
  register your work prior to the infringement, you will need to register
  it prior to filing a suit in federal court).
- If you file it within five years of the first date of publication, it is
  evidence that your copyright is valid.
- You will be able to obtain statutory damages and your attorney fees if
  you register it within three months of the first date of publication or
  prior to the infringement.[199]

It is a much simpler process to register a copyright than a trademark. It may
be useful to copyright material that is of importance to you because of the ability to obtain statutory damages and attorney fees in the event of a lawsuit.
Another benefit of a registered copyright is that you will be able to mention these
types of damages in a cease-and-desist letter. It may help you avoid litigation.

6.13 CAN I REGISTER MY WEBSITE WITH THE COPYRIGHT OFFICE?

Registering web pages is not as easy as it should be, because each updated
version must be registered.[200] What this means is that when you register

your website, you are only protecting the exact copy you provided in your registration. All revisions to your website must be individually registered. Because you probably add information to your website frequently, any new material will not be registered.[201] If you do register the additional information, you are only protecting those specific additions. This is similar to how the Copyright Office treats registration of derivative works (which are works created from previous copyrighted materials).[202] The law regarding copyright has not kept up with website technology.[203] Please note that there are different rules for registering databases and computer programs.

Regardless of this lack of appropriate treatment by the Copyright Office, it is still worth the $35 to register your website. Although your "rights" attach once you put your website in fixed form, the registration provides additional advantages. When you register your copyright, you are putting the world on notice that you claim ownership in your original work. Once registered, you are able to sue for copyright infringement and receive statutory damages and attorney fees if you win. In the case of *Getaped.com, Inc., v. Shelly Cangemi*,[204] the defendants copied the www.getaped.com website and replicated it on their own websites at www.buyaped.com and www.23water.com. After determining that the act of copying the plaintiff's website constituted "publication" under the Copyright Act, the district court ordered the defendants to pay Getaped.com $30,000 in statutory damages plus attorney fees and costs of $16,015. This result occurred because Getaped.com registered the copyright for its website. If Getaped.com had not registered the copyright for its website, it would have only been entitled to its actual damages of $1,050.[205]

There is another important issue regarding website ownership. If you did not design the website yourself and you do not have a written agreement with the designer, the designer may in fact own the copyright to your website. As discussed in question 7.15 (What is a work-for-hire agreement?), the creator of original work is the owner of the copyright, not the person who pays for the work to be created, unless a written agreement to the contrary is in place. In order to register your copyright, you must own the copyright. In order to make sure you do, you will need to have a written agreement with your website designer specifically stating that you own the website and its design and that the designer transfers all copyright ownership, including moral rights, to you. This will allow you to proceed to register your website with the copyright office.

6.14 HOW DO I REGISTER MY WORK WITH THE COPYRIGHT OFFICE?

After you have determined that your work can be registered, you will probably be able to register your copyright with the US Copyright Office without
an attorney.[206] The easiest method is through the Electronic Copyright Office
(eCO) System on the Copyright Office's website.[207] It allows you to register
online, pay a reduced fee of $35, submit your materials online, and pay the
fee online. You will then receive email confirmation of your submission and
will be notified if and when your submission is accepted.[208] You should note
that the Copyright Office has mentioned the possibility of raising this cost to
$65 in the near future.

The Copyright Office explains the process of obtaining a copyright:

Registering a claim to copyright via eCO involves three steps in the
following order:

1. Complete an application
2. Pay the associated fee (pay online with credit/debit card or
   ACH transfer via https://Pay.gov, or with a deposit account)
3. Submit your work[209]

There are different registration forms depending on the type of work you
are registering. For literary works and computer programs you would use
Form TX; for single issue of a periodical you would use Form SE; for a group
of issues of a periodical you would use Form SE/Group; for sound recordings
you would use Form SR; for audio/visual work you would use Form PA; and
for pictorial or graphic works you would use Form VA. You can fill out these
forms and make your payment and upload your work, all of which can be
done online.

If your work includes more than one category, use the form that best fits
the majority of the work. As mentioned in the previous question, if you are
attempting to register a website, you will need to register all of the pages.[210]
As you update your website, you will need to register all substantive changes
to the website to maintain your registration. Similarly, if you register your
blog, you will need to register new posts periodically to maintain your copyright protection.

If you do not wish to submit your application online, you have the option
of mailing it in. In addition to the application, you will submit the fee
(currently $65 for mailed-in copyright applications) and deposits of the

work. For written works that are unpublished, you will provide one copy of the work you are registering. For published works, you will provide two copies. For online works, you can either provide a labeled computer disk containing the work or a printed version of the work. For pictorial or graphic works, you will need to provide two copies. The copies you submit will not be returned. The mailing address is:

Library of Congress Copyright Office
101 Independence Avenue, S.E.
Washington, D.C. 20559-6000

There is an additional weapon you can add to your arsenal if you are concerned about foreign infringement. After you have registered your work with the US Copyright Office, you can then record the registration with the US Customs and Border Protection Office (CBP). This office has an online method for filing initial copyright (and trademark) recordation applications, although renewals must be done through the traditional process. The CBP has the ability to confiscate imported infringing materials.

You will first fill out the electronic application on the CBP website. A separate application is required for each recordation along with a fee of $190 for each copyright registration. You will also be required to file the appropriate supporting documents. For additional information, see the US Customs Service publication called *US Customs & Protection of Intellectual Property Rights.*[211]

6.15 WHAT IS A TRADE SECRET?

A trade secret is any business information that a company wishes to keep confidential and that has economic value because of its secret nature. Trade secret protection attaches by keeping the information secret. You do not register a trade secret. Some companies choose to protect their intellectual property as a trade secret instead of registering a patent, because patent protection lasts only about twenty years. A trade secret lasts as long as you keep it secret.

A trade secret is usually a secret formula, product design, a process, or computer software. Some popular trade secrets are the secret formula for Coca-Cola and Kentucky Fried Chicken's Special Recipe. In order to claim trade secret protection, you must take measures to keep such information secret. If you fail to do so, you will lose your trade secret rights to competitors and/or the public. Generally, you must advise your employees of the secret nature of the information, have those with access to it sign a confidentiality agreement, and limit the number of people who have contact with it. Trade secrets law is governed by state law but is fairly consistent from state to state because most have modeled their laws on the Uniform Trade Secret Act.

The main problem with relying on trade secret status is that once it becomes public knowledge, you no longer have the right to claim trade secret protection. In addition, you have no defense against someone who independently develops your trade secret information.

6.16 HOW LONG DOES TRADE SECRET PROTECTION LAST?

While a patent would provide the most protection against a competitor appropriating your secret information, its protection lasts only twenty years. Trade secret protection lasts as long as you keep it secret. While you can prevent anyone from copying your patent, once a trade secret is made public, you have lost your protection. You can only bring an action against someone who actually stole your secret or violated a confidentiality agreement. You cannot bring a claim against someone who independently developed it.

6.17 HOW DO I PROTECT MY TRADE SECRETS?

You must actively protect your trade secrets in order to receive the protection of the courts. You will need to label your trade secrets as confidential and limit access to them. Most importantly, you should have anyone that will come in contact with the trade secret (including employees) sign a confidentiality agreement (also known as a nondisclosure agreement). These actions are vital because once they become public, you no longer have any protection. You should always make sure that if you are exposing your employees or contractors to information you expect them to keep confidential, you spell out this expectation in writing.

A confidentiality agreement will require anyone who comes in contact with the information to not only keep it secret but also perform certain acts to maintain the secrecy (like shredding copies). In addition to employees, there may be a need to discuss your trade secrets with potential investors, independent contractors, advisors, and lenders. Your agreement should provide that these trade secrets must be kept confidential until such time as they are no longer trade secrets. It is not sufficient to indicate that they will keep the information confidential for two years, as many of these agreements indicate. With a trade secret, the information must be kept confidential until the information is no longer deemed a trade secret.

6.18 WHAT IS A PATENT?

Patent law is exclusively federal law and provides ownership protection for novel, useful, and nonobvious processes, business methods, machines, compositions of matter, inventions, and designs for an article of manufacture. It gives the patent owner the exclusive rights to create, use, sell, and distribute the patented item. Patents are typically valid for twenty years from the date of the filing of the patent application. Although software has been deemed to be patentable under certain conditions by the USPTO, this could change due to a case the Supreme Court is expected to hear soon.[212]

6.19 CAN I PATENT MY WEBSITE?

Although the text of a web page can be copyright protected, it cannot be trademark protected or patented. If you believe you have an invention or business process that could be patented, please refer to www.uspto.gov for more information. Obtaining a patent is an expensive and lengthy process and will require an intellectual property attorney's assistance. Applying for a patent is even more complicated than applying for a trademark.

7 ENFORCING YOUR
INTELLECTUAL PROPERTY RIGHTS

In the case of *Getaped.com, Inc., v. Shelly Cangemi*,[213] the defendants copied the www.getaped.com website and replicated it on their own websites at www.buyaped.com and www.23water.com. After determining that the act of copying the plaintiff's website constituted "publication" under the Copyright Act, the district court ordered the defendants to pay Getaped.com $30,000 in statutory damages plus attorney fees and costs of $16,015. This result occurred because Getaped.com registered the copyright for its website. If Getaped.com had not registered the copyright for its website, it would have only been entitled to its actual damages of $1,050.[214]

Yes, this means that there is an advantage to registering your content with the US Copyright Office. For an investment of $35 for the filing fee, Getaped.com was able to obtain $46,015 in damages—a great deal more than the $1,050 they would have been awarded without registration.

This chapter explains what to do when you believe someone has copied your content without your permission or unlawfully used your name. It spells out the steps to discovering an infringer's identity, what types of correspondence are effective in resolving infringement issues, how to file a takedown notice with an Internet service provider, and what needs to be accomplished before an infringement lawsuit can be filed. It explains the differences between the readers' rights and remedies for copyright infringement and trademark infringement. It also explains why someone may be able to use your work under the fair use exception to infringement.

7.1 WHAT DO I DO IF SOMEONE COPIES MY WORK, WHICH WAS PUBLISHED ON THE INTERNET?

If you believe someone has infringed on your copyright-protected work, you must first determine if the copy was a fair use. Fair use is an exception to copyright infringement that allows others to copy your work in certain situations without your permission. Examples of fair use are reporting, criticism, education, and parody. These exceptions are discussed in detail in question 2.1 (Can I copy information from other websites if I list them as sources?). If you know that you did not give permission for the copied version and do not believe it is a fair use, you will need to obtain evidence of the infringement and discover the identity of the infringer.

First, make copies of the infringing material by saving it in electronic form to your hard drive (not as a link) and printing out a hard copy. Check to see if your copyright notice is intact or if it has been omitted from the copy. You will then need to get information on the infringers. This is discussed in detail in question 7.4 (How do I find out who is infringing on my work?).

You will have a number of options in order to get the infringing material removed and possibly seek damages. These options are discussed in question 7.5 (What do I do after I find out who is infringing on my copyright?). You will also want to make sure that your original work has been registered with the Copyright Office if you think you may need to file a lawsuit. While it is not necessary to register with the copyright office, if you plan on seeking to have the materials removed by contacting the Internet service provider hosting the infringing material, it makes it a lot easy to prove copyright ownership if you have the certificate from the Copyright Office. In addition, make sure that your most recent registration includes the material that has been copied. This is especially important if you only register updates periodically. Remember, you cannot obtain statutory damages or attorney fees without registration.

7.2 WHAT IS FAIR USE?

Fair use is considered noninfringing, permissible copying of copyrighted material without the owner's consent. Determining fair use is not clear-cut. There is a balancing of factors, including the work's purpose, the amount copied, the nature of the work, and its effect on the marketplace. Examples of fair use include criticism, comment, reporting, educational use, and parody.

The purpose of the use is one of the most important factors in determining fair use. Courts will look to see if the original copyrighted work was modified to create the allegedly infringing work or if instead it was simply copied. This is known as a derivative work (when a new piece of work is created from a former one). In other words, it is less likely to be a fair use if someone copies your work, makes a couple of changes, and then posts it as his or her own than if the person reposted your work verbatim in a blog post and criticized it. In addition, an unauthorized commercial use is more likely to be found infringing than an informational use. If someone copies an image you created and uses it as his or her logo, this will not be considered fair use. Copying your image and commenting on it could be.

A court is more likely to find infringement when the nature of the original copyrighted work is fictional. It is assumed that fictional works are more creative and original than nonfictional works. This is because there are only so many ways to state facts. Similar wording of nonfiction information is more likely to be fair use. If you have several reporters all reporting the same event, there will be some overlap in the terms and descriptions used.

An unauthorized use will probably be considered a fair use if only a small amount or percentage of the original work has been used. For example, if you republish an entire blog post made by someone else, this would more likely be designated as infringement than if you merely quoted a sentence or two and commented on it in your own post. Fair use allows you to use small portions of others' work.

When the unauthorized use actually competes with the copyright owner's work in the marketplace, resulting in decreased sales, a court will usually find that the use was not a fair use. When a musical piece is found to contain a similar series of chords to an already published piece, for example, this could have a negative impact on sales of the original piece because songs are deemed to compete with one another in the marketplace. If you quoted some lyrics in your post, it would not be deemed to be competing with the sale of the song in the marketplace.

Because these fair use factors are very subjective, courts have made rulings that seem inconsistent with one another. You should use your judgment when reviewing work on the Internet that seems to be an actual copy or derivative work of yours. Just because someone claims to be using it for fair use does not mean a judge will agree. Nor does every copy of your work constitute infringement. For example, if a blogger mentions in one of his posts something he read on your blog, this may very well be considered reporting, comment, or criticism—all of which are fair uses. The steps to take when confronted with an actual infringement are discussed in question 7.5 (What do I do after I find out who is infringing on my copyright?).

Copyright law attempts to achieve a balance between the public's right to copy or otherwise use someone else's materials and the creator's right to profit from his or her own work. I am hoping that we will see changes in copyright law that will better define what constitutes fair use and reduce the penalties for minor noncommercial infringement (such as downloading a song for personal use). Currently, organizations such as the Motion Picture Association of America and the Recording Industry Association of America are using the Copyright Act's steep penalties to punish those who copy or post any portion of copyrighted movies or music, even if the use is not commercial. Most people do not feel that the judgment amounts (due to statutory damages) are justified in these situations. Public outrage over some of these suits and the new push for open-source software and other creative commons rights are changing society's opinion from one that seeks to protect the creator's rights to one that honors the public's rights to information on the Internet.[215]

7.3 WHAT DO I DO IF SOMEONE COPIES THE LOOK AND FEEL OF MY WEBSITE?

Because there are so many form websites out there, many websites do in fact look similar. A copyright infringement issue arises when you create (or contract with someone to create) a unique web design with unique features that is copied by someone else. Remember that before you can bring a suit in federal court, you must register your copyright. By registering your website with the Copyright Office, you will have protection for the exact pages registered. The issue becomes whether your website was actually copied. While some courts easily find that any website is accessible to anyone else, others have required a showing that the infringer actually viewed and copied the website. The easiest way to show that copying did occur is by showing that the source code for the two websites is identical. As you can imagine, this situation usually is a result of contracting out your web design. Unless you specifically spell out in a written agreement that you own the web design, the entity that created your website will own the copyright to the design and have the right to use it for someone else.

There have been some who have made a claim for trade dress infringement, indicating that the "look and feel" of a website is actually trade dress. In *Blue Nile, Inc. v. Ice.com, Inc.*,[216] Blue Nile sued Ice.com for copying the overall "look and feel" of its jewelry website. After the court denied Ice.com's motion to dismiss and ruled that a claim for trade dress infringement based on the look and feel of the website could proceed, the parties settled. Although the exact nature of this claim has yet to be resolved, it does seem that, since a website can be copyright protected and the appearance of a website would seem to fall under trade dress, claims such as these may be brought.

7.4 HOW DO I FIND OUT WHO IS INFRINGING ON MY WORK?

If the infringing material is located on a private website, you can look on the site to see if there is an email address or hard address listed. If you can find the name of the owner on the website, you can do a Google search to find the person's address. Another option is to search the website's "who is" information. You can do this on www.godaddy.com or www.whois.net. If the infringing material appears on a hosted site, such as Facebook or YouTube, you will have an option to request that the material be taken down by the Internet service provider. If it appears in the comments made to a blog, you may contact the blogger or the hosting company of the blog. Your ability to seek relief will depend on where the infringing material is republished.

If you need to bring an action against an infringer and cannot locate his or her identity, it is possible to obtain a subpoena for the owner's identity.

7.5 WHAT DO I DO AFTER I FIND OUT WHO IS INFRINGING ON MY COPYRIGHT?

You should probably begin by asking for proper credit to be given to your work. You can accomplish this by writing a demand letter informing the infringer that you are aware of the violation but wish to resolve it amicably by permitting him or her to add your copyright notice (and whatever other information you desire, such as a link to your website or blog). You will need to give the person a deadline and ask for confirmation in writing of his or her compliance. Depending on the type of work copied, you may inform the person of his or her ability to continue to post your content for a fee (this is called a license agreement).

The next easiest course of action may be to take advantage of the Digital Millennium Copyright Act (DMCA) of 1998.[217] In fact, some people go straight to this step. The main thrust of the DMCA is (1) to provide a limitation on liability for Internet service providers (ISPs), (2) to prohibit circumventing antipiracy software, and (3) to require that rebroadcasters of copyrighted material on the Internet pay for using the copyrighted materials. Before enactment of the DMCA, ISPs were the target of many copyright infringement suits. An ISP is defined as "a provider of online services or network access, or the operator of facilities therefor." The DMCA provides that ISPs may be shielded from liability arising out of copyright infringement if they can meet certain requirements. So although you may not sue an ISP, if you believe you have been infringed upon, you can get the ISP to remove infringing uses of your work by following the procedures described below.

Because of the immunity the DCMA provides ISPs, they generally follow the procedures set forth in the DMCA. First, you would send a takedown notice to the applicable ISP (see question 7.6—How do I file a takedown notice?). In the notice you will need to identify yourself as the copyright owner, identify the copyrighted work claimed to be infringed, and identify the website that is infringing on the work. You should also include your contact information and a statement that the complaint is made in "good faith," and you should also verify that the information contained in the notification is accurate.[218]

A takedown notice is different from a cease-and-desist letter. A cease-and-desist letter is sent to the actual infringer, whereas the takedown notice is sent to the website owner or Internet service provider where the infringing material appears. Most takedown notices, if they meet the statutes requirements, result in the removal of the infringing material. You should be aware that if you do not meet the statutes requirements and are found to be attempting to harass the person who you believe is infringing on your work (or otherwise send the takedown notice in bad faith), you could be subject to an anti-SLAPP suit in some states. These actions are discussed in questions 1.5 (Don't anti-SLAPP laws protect me?) and 2.12 (What do I do if I receive a takedown notice?).

If you do decide to go to court, you will first need to register your work with the copyright office. This will allow you to file in a US Court and seek statutory damages and attorney fees.[219] In most cases you will have three years from the date of infringement to file your suit, but please check with an attorney as soon as you discover the infringement to determine exactly how the statute of limitations applies to your specific facts. Prior to filing suit, you should send a cease-and-desist letter to the infringer. In this letter you will demand that the infringer remove the offending material or be subject to a lawsuit. Do not send a cease-and-desist letter if you have no intention of going to court as you will have then put yourself in the position of acknowledging the infringement and by your actions letting the infringer know that you will do nothing about it. This will open the door for future infringements.

The suit will have to be filed in the federal district court as opposed to your local state court. If you do not register your work with the Copyright Office, you may only recover actual damages.[220] Please note that when the infringer removes your copyright notice, it is easier to prove that the infringement was willful, entitling you to enhanced statutory damages. It is extremely important to register your copyright before an infringement so that you can get attorney fees and statutory damages from an infringer. Because actual damages may be difficult to prove, it is desirable to be able to go for statutory damages. With a registered copyright, the court can award statutory damages to the infringer of up to $30,000 for each copyrighted work infringed. If the infringement was willful, the court can award statutory damages up to $150,000. In the *Getaped.com* case above, the plaintiff was able to obtain a judgment for statutory damages of $30,000 plus attorneys' fees and costs of $16,015 for a total of $46,015 in damages.

7.6 HOW DO I FILE A TAKEDOWN NOTICE?

Before you send off a cease-and-desist letter, you need to remember that people can make copies of your work under the fair use exception. As discussed above, whether their use will be considered fair use depends on a number of factors: (1) How unique was the original work? (2) Was the copy used for commercial purposes? (3) What portion of the original work was copied? (4) Did the copy reduce the demand for the original work in the marketplace? If someone copies a large portion of your online work for his or her own commercial purposes, your work was very unique, and the copy is diverting readers or customers from your site, you will probably be able to claim infringement against that person. On the other hand, if he or she is merely quoting something from your content and commenting on it, it would probably be considered a fair use.

If you have contacted the poster of the infringing material and have either received no response or the person does not agree to remove the infringing material, you can file a takedown notice under the DMCA. The notice should be sent to the designated agent for the website (or ISP) where the material is posted. A list of designated agents is maintained by the US Copyright Office, but this information should also be located on the website, usually in its terms of use or DMCA policy. In addition, a takedown notice must contain the following items in order to be valid:

Elements of notification.—

To be effective under this subsection, a notification of claimed infringement must be a written communication provided to the designated agent of a service provider that includes substantially the following:

(i) A physical or electronic signature of a person authorized to act on behalf of the owner of an exclusive right that is allegedly infringed.

(ii) Identification of the copyrighted work claimed to have been infringed, or, if multiple copyrighted works at a single online site are covered by a single notification, a representative list of such works at that site.

(iii) Identification of the material that is claimed to be infringing or to be the subject of infringing activity and that is to be removed or access to which is to be disabled, and information reasonably sufficient to permit the service provider to locate the material.

(iv) Information reasonably sufficient to permit the service provider to contact the complaining party, such as an address, telephone number, and, if available, an electronic mail address at which the complaining party may be contacted.

(v) A statement that the complaining party has a good faith belief that use of the material in the manner complained of is not authorized by the copyright owner, its agent, or the law.

(vi) A statement that the information in the notification is accurate, and under penalty of perjury, that the complaining party is authorized to act on behalf of the owner of an exclusive right that is allegedly infringed.[221]

The DMCA requires the owner of the website or ISP to remove the offending material upon your request. If that person fails to do so, he will lose his immunity from a lawsuit. If the person who originally posted the material files a counter-notice, the website owner or ISP will notify you, and you will have fourteen business days to file a lawsuit and notify the service provider that you have done so, or else the service provider is obligated to put the disputed material back up.[222]

7.7 WHAT CAN I DO IF SOMEONE INFRINGES ON MY DOMAIN NAME?

If someone uses your domain name with a different extension, you do have some rights. The Anticybersquatting Act is discussed in question 6.7 (What is cybersquatting?). Essentially, cybersquatting occurs when someone uses your domain name or trade name in bad faith. You will run into problems if someone's use is deemed a parody or if that use is innocent. In other words, if someone with a similar business registers a similar name, and it appears that there is no attempt to divert customers from your website, this would not be deemed cybersquatting. However, if someone is using your actual trade name in his or her domain name, you could proceed to enforce your trademark rights under the ICANN's Uniform Domain Name Dispute Resolution Policy (UDRP) or the Anticybersquatting Consumer Protection Act (ACPA).

If you find that someone is using your trademark in his or her domain name wrongfully, as a first step, you may want to consider seeking relief through ICANN's UDRP. ICANN is the organization responsible for the coordination of the global Internet's systems of unique identifiers. ICANN manages the top-level domain names. ICANN is charged with the duty of resolving disputes among top-level domain names. When you register a domain name, you agree to be bound by the UDRP, which spells out the procedures for arbitrating these disputes.

To succeed with a UDRP claim, you would need to show that the infringing use is likely to confuse the public (as you would with a federal lawsuit) and is done in bad faith. UDRP is an arbitration proceeding that is generally less expensive and much quicker than a court proceeding. Using ICANN's UDRP process tends to be both quicker and less expensive.

Essentially, an arbitration panel will hear your complaint. You will be required to show that: (1) you have trademark rights in the original mark, (2) the offending domain name is identical or similar enough to cause a likelihood of confusion, (3) the alleged cybersquatter is not using it as a fair use and does not have your permission to use it, and (4) the alleged cybersquatter registered the domain name in bad faith. Bad faith can usually be established by showing that the cybersquatter bought it intending to sell it to you or take advantage of the confusion to draw customers to his or her site instead of yours.

If you do not prevail in the UDRP proceedings, you can still file in federal court for trademark infringement. Even though you cannot win a damage award, you will be able to stop the infringer from using the offending name and can have the name transferred to you.

The ACPA[223] prohibits the registering, selling, or using of a domain name confusingly similar to, or dilutive of, a trademark or service mark. The advantage of the ACPA over the UDRP is that it does permit a damage award. To prove that someone is cybersquatting, you must show that the infringing domain name is identical or confusingly similar to you trademark and that the infringer has "a bad faith intent to profit from that mark." If your trademark is additionally deemed a "famous" mark, such as Coca-Cola, you can prevent an infringer from "diluting" your trademark. Dilution occurs when someone uses a famous mark. You do not have to show a likelihood of confusion. It is assumed that the use will harm the famous mark.

The ACPA covers typosquatting, which involves registering misspellings of domain names of popular trademarks in order to divert traffic that would ordinarily go to their site to another site. If someone is found to have typosquatted, the court can order the cancellation of the offending domain name or transfer it to the holder of the trademark. You can also recover up to three times your actual damages or opt for statutory damages of up to $100,000 per offending domain name. You can also get a court order issued that will stop the offender from using the typosquatting name.

7.8 WHAT CAN I DO IF SOMEONE USES MY TRADE NAME WITHOUT MY CONSENT?

If you believe someone has infringed upon your trademark, you have a number of options. For there to be infringement, there has to be an infringing use that is likely to confuse the public. In order to have common-law trademark rights, your trademark must have been used in commerce and be distinctive. To be used in commerce means it has to actually be shown to the public in connection with your business. As previously noted, trademark protection attaches as soon as it is used in commerce. Federal registration is not necessary but will offer certain benefits in the event of a lawsuit. The reason for the distinctiveness requirement is that the value in a trademark is the consumers' association of it with your particular business.

Section 32 of the Lanham Act provides federal protection for registered marks if the infringer "uses in commerce" another's mark "in connection with the sale . . . of any goods or services . . . [where] such use is likely to cause confusion [among consumers]."[224] Section 43(a) of the Lanham Act also protects unregistered marks by holding an infringer liable for "using in commerce" another's mark "on or in connection with any goods or services" where such use is likely to cause confusion among consumers "as to the origin, sponsorship, or approval" of the infringer's "goods, services, or commercial activities."[225] Unregistered trademarks are also protected by state law.[226]

The Lanham Act was amended in 1999 to provide protection for domain names as trademarks. The Lanham Act provides relief for a variety of trademark issues, such as trademark infringement, trademark dilution, and false advertising. To bring suit under the Lanham Act, there are eight factors courts may consider in determining whether a likelihood of confusion exists between the goods or services:

- Strength of the mark;
- Proximity or relatedness of the goods;
- Similarity of the marks (especially in sight, sound and meaning);
- Evidence of actual confusion;
- Marketing channels;
- Type of goods and purchaser care (meaning how much care does a purchaser take before buying the product);
- Intent when choosing the mark; and
- Likelihood of expansion of the product lines.[227]

The important thing about trademarks is that you lose the protection of the law if you fail to enforce your rights. This means that you must actively pursue legitimate infringement claims against those who would divert consumers to their business or dilute the value of your products or services.

7.9 WHAT ELSE CAN I DO TO PROTECT MY NAME FROM INFRINGEMENT?

There are a number of steps you can take to help protect yourself from infringers. Having said that, please understand that it is very easy for people to copy things off the Internet. You have to be diligent in enforcing your rights, which is becoming increasingly more difficult. In one case I handled, I did a Google search on my client's domain name and came up with over 250,000 hits. Not all of the links were to her site. As mentioned, the law requires you to monitor your intellectual property so that you can stop infringers. I imagine this responsibility will have to shift somewhat as courts begin to realize what an impossible task it is to "monitor" the Internet. There is no one who can view 250,000 hits each and every day seeking out the needle in the haystack that actually constitutes infringement. What this means is at a minimum that when the infringement is brought to your attention, you need to deal with it.

7.10 IF I DO NEED TO SUE SOMEONE, CAN I DO IT IN MY LOCAL COURTHOUSE?

In order to bring a lawsuit against someone, the court must have jurisdiction over the person you are suing. A defendant (the person you are suing) has to have sufficient contacts with the state in which you are suing him or her. In other words, if you purchase an iPod from someone in Michigan and you live in Texas, unless the seller does a good amount of business in Texas, it is unlikely that you will be able to obtain jurisdiction over the seller in a Texas court. A single Internet transaction is usually not enough.[228] However, if you are suing someone based on his or her interaction with your website and you have a "forum selection clause" in your terms of use indicating that any lawsuits against you must be brought in your home state and that any actions that you take against a customer can be brought in your home state, this could be enforceable.[229] Opinions in different states on jurisdiction issues have varied.

A New York judge[230] held AOL's forum selection clause unenforceable against small claims. In balancing the interests of the company and the wronged individual, the judge indicated that interests established in small claims cases (easy access and low cost to litigants) outweighed AOL's interest in defending lawsuits in its jurisdiction.

A judge in New York[231] upheld Match.com's forum selection clause, which stated that all lawsuits against it had to be filed in Northern Texas. In this case, the users of Match.com were required to check a box indicating that they agreed to the Match.com terms of use. The first sentence of the terms of use indicated, "If you object to anything in this agreement. . ., do not use the Website or Service." Within the terms of use was the subject forum selection clause. The court found that the forum selection clause had been reasonably communicated and that since Match.com was located in Northern Texas, without offices in any other states, it was reasonable for the company to add that type of clause so that it would not be subject to lawsuits in the other forty-nine states. The court specifically stated that had there not been a forum selection clause, Match.com would have been subject to suit in all fifty states.

Remember, in this case the users had to click to agree to the terms of use. The result may have been different had the forum selection clause had been buried in lengthy terms of use or in terms of use that were difficult to locate on the website.

As discussed in Chapter 9, binding terms of use on your website can address the issue of jurisdiction in your favor. Without indicating where lawsuits may be brought, a plaintiff anywhere in the world could file suit against you based on his or her interaction with your website. This means that you could have to defend yourself in another state or country. Because your website can be viewed by people anywhere, it is important to make sure this issue is addressed before putting your website online. With respect to a lawsuit you bring against someone else, it is always preferable to bring it locally. Whether or not you will be able to obtain jurisdiction over that defendant depends on your state's long-arm statute.

If there is not a forum selection clause in the terms of use, the court will look to see if the defendant had sufficient contacts with the state in which the defendant is being sued. In the 2010 case of *Grimaldi v. Guinn*,[232] a New York plaintiff sued a Pennsylvania defendant in New York under New York law due to damage caused to the plaintiff's 1969 Camaro, on which the defendants had worked. The New York Court of Appeals, affirming the lower court, held that although an informational website viewed by those in the State of New York is not sufficient to gain jurisdiction over the business with the website, "if a Web site provides information, permits access to e-mail communication, describes the goods or services offered, downloads a printed order form, or allows online sales with the use of a credit card, and sales are, in fact, made ... then the assertion of personal jurisdiction may be reasonable." In *Grimaldi v. Guinn*, the court ruled that if you have an informational website, the court will look to the totality of the circumstances in deciding whether there is jurisdiction over the defendants. Specifically, the court looked at "the number, nature and timing of all of the contacts involved, including the numerous telephone, fax, e-mail, and other written communications with the plaintiff in New York that Guinn initiated subsequent to his initial involvement in the project, as well as the manner in which Guinn employed his decidedly passive Web site for commercial access, Guinn must be deemed to have sufficient contacts with this State."

There have been a number of defamation cases in which courts have not found personal jurisdiction over defendants. In *Brayton Purcell LLP v. Recordon Recordon*,[233] the federal court held that even though the defendant knew where the plaintiff resided, it was not sufficient for jurisdiction purposes involving an intentional tort (like defamation). While some feel that the law of the state where the person who made the defamatory statement resides should apply (because presumably that is the law which was relied upon in making the statement), others feel that the victims of such torts are further harmed when they cannot bring an action in their local courthouse.

Essentially, this means that if you have a cause of action against someone, you will be able to bring that action at your local courthouse if the person or entity you are suing has "sufficient contacts" with your state. Where you bring the lawsuit will also depend on whether you are suing under federal or state laws. If you want to file a copyright infringement case, you will need to bring it in federal court. If you are bringing a breach of contract case based on your state's laws, your local court will be more appropriate. If you are suing someone based on contact with your website or blog which has terms of use indicating that all actions will be brought in your local jurisdiction, this may be enforceable.[234]

7.11 HOW DO I LICENSE MY INTELLECTUAL PROPERTY?

A copyright owner of a work, such as a blog post, can grant permission for others to use it. When you maintain ownership of your work and just desire to allow someone else to use it, you can enter into a license agreement with such a party. The main reason for licensing your intellectual property is to receive payment from others using your work.

A license is a legal agreement giving permission for someone to use your work under the conditions you set forth in exchange for payment (either one-time or on a periodic basis lasting as long as the time granted in the license). A license can be exclusive, meaning you agree that you are only permitting this one entity to use your work, or nonexclusive, meaning you can sign multiple license agreements with multiple entities. A license is different from a complete transfer or sale of your work in that you maintain ownership when you license it. If you transfer all of your rights, you have given up your ownership of the intellectual property.

I should mention here that in addition to granting a license to someone in exchange for money, there may be some reasons for you to dedicate your work to the public domain or enter into a Creative Commons license.[235] The biggest difference between the outright selling of your work and licensing it is that when you sell it you no longer have the right to use it. When you license it, you can specifically carve out what you are keeping and what you are granting. The factors you would consider are the potential for making money down the line from the work, the extent of control you wish to retain over the work, and the costs involved in licensing the work.

7.12 HOW DO I SELL MY INTELLECTUAL PROPERTY?

There are situations in which you will desire to actually transfer ownership of your intellectual property. Sometimes this is called an assignment of rights. First, if you ever work as an independent contractor and create content, a website, or artwork for someone else, unless that person has requested a written agreement from you, you will own the intellectual property. The same is true when you hire someone to help you. Always obtain a written agreement spelling out who owns what. Second, there may come a time when you wish to sell your website, blog, or business. Your most important asset will be your intellectual property. You must make sure that you can grant title to it. This is discussed in question 3.4 (Who owns the content that I post about someone else's products or services?). Essentially, a sale of intellectual property should release you from further liability unless you are paid to agree otherwise.

7.13 HOW DO I KEEP TRACK OF MY INTELLECTUAL PROPERTY?

You are probably now realizing that you have a lot of intellectual property. Not only should you properly protect it but you should also make sure that you keep all of the rights you have in it (and keep track of others' permitted uses). Not only will this be of value if you ever need to enforce your rights but it can also be a valuable asset if you ever seek to sell your Internet presence to a third party. Such buyers will want to be assured that you actually own what you claim to own and that you have the ability to transfer all of the rights in your name, logo, work, domain name, etc., to them.

You should begin by documenting all of your intellectual property. You will need to list the dates that all of your work was created and published, and make copies of state and federal registrations. Start by labeling a file folder for each item in which you claim an intellectual property right. In each folder you should include the following:

- A copy of the actual work
- The dates of creation and publication

- Any federal or state filing made
- Information about the creation of the work, such as the name of the author (and copies of any independent contractor agreements, if applicable)
- Any license agreements relating to the work
- Evidence of continuous use in the case of a trade name

It is especially important that you maintain written agreements with any nonemployee who creates work for you. With an employee, it is safest to have a written employment agreement documenting that anything created while working for you is the property of the business (but courts will generally assume this in employment situations). Please note that in any event, the written agreement or employment status must be in advance of the creation of the work. If this is not the case, you will need an actual transfer document granting title in the work to you from its creator.

7.14 WHAT TYPES OF AGREEMENTS WILL I NEED TO PROTECT MY INTELLECTUAL PROPERTY?

Any attorney will tell you that every agreement you enter into (that you may need to enforce at some time) should be in writing; this is especially true with respect to your intellectual property. Such documents could include your employment agreements, independent contractor agreements, work-for-hire agreements, confidentiality agreements, and license agreements.

A contract will specifically spell out what is expected of both sides. It should be clear, complete, and easy to understand. First, if you desire to post any information online that you did not create yourself, you need a written agreement with the creator giving you the rights in the content. This includes a web design agreement, a web hosting agreement, and a web development agreement. If you have employees, make sure that your written agreement indicates that any work they create on your behalf (or while in your employ, depending on the circumstances) belongs to you. If you use independent contractors to create content, provide photos, develop graphics, or write text, you must have a written acknowledgement that the content belongs to you. This is discussed in further detail in question 7.15.

7.15 WHAT IS A WORK-FOR-HIRE AGREEMENT?

First of all, works made by an employee for an employer will automatically belong to the employer. The Copyright Act defines these creations by an employee as a work-for-hire. When you use an independent contractor, as opposed to an employee, to create content, a website, or other intellectual property for you, the worker will not be considered a work-for-hire unless your agreement is in writing. If you fail to obtain a written agreement, the work will belong to the independent contractor. The agreement with the independent contractor should, at a minimum, spell out in specificity what is being created, the price for the creation, and the time within which the creation must be completed, and it should not only transfer the title to you but also indicate that the independent contractor has the right to do so and warrants that he or she has not infringed on anyone else's rights in creating the work. If you do not spell this out in the independent contractor agreement, make sure you obtain a written document transferring ownership of the work to you before you pay for it.

8 LEGAL ISSUES TO CONSIDER
WHEN SETTING UP A WEBSITE

In *National Federation of the Blind, et al. v Target Corporation*,[236] Target was sued because its retail website, Target.com, was not accessible to those with visual impairments, allegedly in violation of the Americans with Disabilities Act. Although the organization's motion for a mandatory injunction to require Target to make its site accessible was denied, the court indicated that the Federation could proceed with its lawsuit. In 2008, Target agreed to settle by paying $6 million to the Federation and agreeing to modify its website with the input of the Federation. In addition, Target was ordered to reimburse the National Federation of the Blind its attorney fees and costs of $3,738,864.96.[237]

This case was considered unusual at the time because previous courts had held that websites were not "public accommodations" under the ADA. Although this case was settled, Target must have felt that it did not have a chance of winning or that the negative publicity it would have encountered would have cost the company more than $6 million.[238] There have been a number of cases involving this issue since that time. The Department of Justice website notes that it is currently seeking to update its ADA standards to require websites to be accessible.[239] Regardless, website owners should make sure that they understand what their responsibilities are to those with disabilities and be prepared for changes in the law.

This chapter will discuss the various issues that arise when first setting up a website in terms of ownership, content, and purpose. It explains the types of agreements to include on the website regarding the ownership and use of content, what risks are involved in using content that the owner did not create, and the prohibitions on certain types of content and online activities. It addresses when contracts that are entered into over the Internet are legal and some of the legal issues involved in e-commerce. It also discusses how website owners and bloggers can be held liable for the actions of third parties who post defamatory comments, links, or infringing content on their websites or blogs, or who hack into and steal the private information of users of a website or blog and how to lessen those risks.

8.1 IS IT SAFER TO SET UP MY OWN SITE OR POST ON OTHERS' SITES?

There are a number of inherent risks in setting up a website. These include liability for infringement, torts, breach of contract, and violations of federal and state law. Remember, ignorance of the law is no excuse. While you cannot be expected to know every law of every state, you can have an action brought against you for violating a statute that you were not aware of.

The following are ways to avoid or lessen some of the most common risks encountered by website owners. Terms of use and privacy policies are discussed more fully in Chapter 9 but will be briefly touched upon here.

Terms of use. As I mentioned in my introduction, when my business clients started developing their own websites around ten years ago, they did not contact me for legal advice. They just assumed they could copy from other websites freely. Many would just take the terms of use from a well-known site and copy and paste them as their own. My clients are a little savvier now, I hope. Whenever you create a website or blog, by incorporating terms of use, you have set up what users can expect from you and what you expect from them. It is essentially a contract regarding Internet usage with respect to your website.

Privacy policy. Copying a privacy policy from another website poses even bigger risks. As mentioned in Chapter 4, the FTC comes down hard on those who violate their own privacy policies. If you have a policy that you did not create, chances are you are doing something completely different with your users' information than you have represented. It is very important to accurately describe what you do with users' information and to provide them with a chance to opt out of your collection and dissemination of their information. You may also need to add additional provisions to your privacy policy if (1) you do business in California, (2) you have users under the age of thirteen, or (3) you are in certain industries, such as financial or medical.

Infringement. Using someone else's materials or trademarks without his or her consent can result in an infringement lawsuit. While you may have protection from infringing posts made by third parties, you are liable for what you post yourself. Unless you are certain your use falls under the fair use exception or you have written consent to use the materials, do not copy someone else's work onto your website. It is not enough to give that person credit—it is still infringement even if you indicate where you found the information.

FTC Endorsement Guides. If you are posting on your own website about a product or service, you need to make truthful posts and identify your relationship with the product or service provider. For example, if you blog about how great a certain moisturizer is and you received a free jar in the mail, you must disclose that. Similarly, if you permit others to post on your website in the way of testimonials about your services or products, the same rules apply. The testimonials must be truthful and not misleading, and any relationship between the person making the testimonial and yourself must be disclosed.

Security. As discussed in Chapter 4, website owners can be found liable for security breaches. It is recommended that you use standard industry precautions to keep all data collected safe. If you collect credit card or other financial information, you should not store it on your computer. You should also seek professional assistance in order to comply with the Payment Card Industry Data Security Standards. In addition, each state has its own data security laws that you need to be aware of in addition to any industry-specific data security requirements.

Immunity statutes. There are two statutes that provide immunity to websites and ISPs for material posted by third parties which may alleviate some of the concerns. These are the Digital Millennium Copyright Act (DMCA) and the Communications Decency Act (CDA).

In order to receive protection under the DMCA, you should designate an agent to receive any DMCA takedown notices, notify the copyright office of your agent, post the takedown notice procedures on your website along with the contact information of the designated agent, and the action you may take against repeat offenders. When you receive a takedown notice, you must respond promptly. This requires the website owner or ISP to remove the infringing material, notify the poster that it has been removed, notify the copyright owner if a counter-notice is received, and repost pursuant to the counter-notice if the copyright owner does not inform you within fourteen business days that he or she will be filing suit.

The DMCA immunity provisions apply only to claims of copyright infringement. They do not apply to trademark infringement claims. However, because there is no immunity for website owners or ISPs for trademark infringement, you should probably remove any alleged infringing materials upon request. In some cases, you may have immunity against tort claims, such as defamation, as provided in Section 230 of the Communications Decency Act. Remember, the immunity is only with respect to third-party posts; it does not apply to posts made by you.

8.2 IF I CREATE THE WEBSITE, BLOG, OR FACEBOOK PAGE, DO I OWN IT?

If you or your employee created the site, you own it. If it was created by an independent contractor or web designer, you will need a written agreement transferring ownership of the site to you. If you have an oral agreement, your independent contractor or web designer will have a copyright ownership in your website. In addition, users who make posts on your website own their own comments. You will not be able to republish these comments elsewhere, unless it is fair use (like reporting or criticism). What this means is that you need a written agreement with anyone who creates content for your site giving ownership to you or a license to you with the ability to modify, delete, and republish the materials. You should also have terms of use on your site that permit you to do the same. By putting these agreements in place, you will own the content on your website.

As discussed in Chapter 5, there are a number of current lawsuits between employers and former employees over the ownership of Twitter followers, Twitter handles, Facebook pages, Facebook passwords, and a slew of other ownership disputes. The courts will most likely find that companies with written agreements as to the ownership of social media accounts will fare better than those without. If you are a social media marketer who takes a job as an employee for a company, you want to make sure you have a written employment agreement maintaining ownership of all of your social media accounts and followers. You do not want to be in a position of fighting with a former employer over who owns your followers (especially if you have spent a great deal of time and effort creating your following). Likewise, a company may want to make sure that if you are doing social media work for them, they own their company pages, handles, and followers. (This should not be a conflict provided their business is not social media marketing!)

8.3 CAN I POST CONTENT THAT I DID NOT CREATE?

If you or an employee created the content on the site, you own it. However, if you want to add content that you did not create, you will need to make sure that you have obtained the proper releases or licenses to use such materials on your site. If you are using content made by an independent contractor for your site, you will need a written agreement transferring title of such copyrighted work to you as discussed in question 7.15 (What is a work-for-hire agreement?).

If you see something on another site that you want to add to yours, you can request permission from the site owner. Many times the owner will be happy to grant permission if you credit the source and/or provide a link to his or her site. The beauty of the Internet is the ability to link similar sites. If your site winds up getting a lot of traffic, the sites you link to will benefit from that as well. You will run across situations in which permission is denied or you receive no response. In that case, move on. There are many items you can copy onto your website without the risks of infringement listed in question 2.2 (Can I copy work that is in the public domain?) and question 2.5 (Can I copy and/or email reports and information from government websites?). If you copy something from another source without permission, whether or not you give the owner credit, you could be liable for infringement as discussed in question 2.1 (Can I copy information from other websites if I list them as sources?).

The courts have split on whether or not linking to an internal page on someone else's website without permission constitutes contributory infringement. A hyperlink or link is an underlined phrase on a website that you click to direct you to another website. The court in *Ticketmaster Corp. v. Tickets. com, Inc.*[240] held that the deep links in this case did not constitute infringement because there was no "copying." The court seemed to imply that because the material was not copied to Ticket.com's site and the users knew that they were being directed to someone else's website, this did not constitute infringement. In this case, the linking website actually stated that the users were being directed to another website to purchase tickets there. This is contrary to the decision in *Live Nation Motor Sports, Inc. v. Davis*,[241] which held that linking to webcasts of motocross races that were located on Live Nation's website did constitute infringement because Davis's site was "copying" (in violation of the Copyright Act) webcasts from Live Nation's site without permission. Thus, the deep links did constitute infringement.

8.4 AM I LIABLE FOR WHAT OTHER PEOPLE POST ON MY SITE?

As discussed earlier, there are situations in which you can become liable for what someone else has posted on your website. Although you have some protection under the Digital Millennium Copyright Act for copyright infringement issues, and the Communications Decency Act for tort issues, there are a number of situations that these two statutes do not cover. Nor will you have protection if you do not follow all of their procedures and each subsection of the statutes.

Contributory copyright infringement occurs when you in some way assisted or encouraged someone else's infringement. If you edit what others post, then you are more likely to be found liable for contributory infringement. If you have a blog or Facebook page and you do not edit what others post, you are in a better position to argue against contributory infringement or vicarious liability. Vicarious liability attaches when you become liable for what someone else does because of your ability to control what this person does (such as with an employee).

The courts again are split on whether or not a website can be liable for offending user-generated content (outside of the areas of the DMCA and CDA). For example, trademark infringement is not protected under either of these statutes. However, the trend seems to be to attach liability to the website only when the website has received notice of the infringement and fails to remove it.

In *Inwood Laboratories, Inc. v. Ives Laboratories, Inc.*,[242] the Supreme Court set the test for determining contributory trademark infringement. The owner of the trademark must prove either that the defendant "intentionally induce[d] another to infringe a trademark" or that he or she "continue[d] to supply the infringing products" after receiving notice that it was "engaging in trademark infringement." In *Tiffany v. eBay*,[243] the court refused to hold the auction website liable for selling counterfeit goods and stated that Tiffany had the obligation of policing its own trademark. In this case eBay did remove the infringing post after being notified that it constituted infringement. Similarly, in *Sellify v. Amazon.com* [244] the court found that Amazon, as an online merchant, could not be held liable for contributory infringement for the trademark infringement of one of its affiliates because Amazon neither posted the content nor was the infringer an agent of Amazon. In this case, Amazon did remove the affiliate from the program after receiving notice of the alleged infringement. Compare this with *Gucci Am., Inc. v. Hall & Assocs. and Mindspring Enter., Inc.*,[245] where the court denied the ISP's motion to dismiss the contributory trademark infringement claim because the ISP had received numerous notifications of the trademark infringement and failed to act. This case also held that the Communications Decency Act did not provide immunity for the ISP in infringement actions.

Vicarious infringement requires a different analysis. Vicarious liability attaches when a website has the right and ability to control the infringer, such as with an employee, and receives a financial benefit from the infringement. The DMCA provides no immunity for vicarious copyright infringement. Similarly, vicarious trademark infringement has been found to exist in a number of cases. In *Louis Vuitton Malletier, S.A. v. Akanoc Solutions, Inc.*,[246] the web hosting company was ordered to pay Louis Vuitton $31 million in damages after finding the web hosting company liable for contributory copyright and trademark infringement. The reason was that it failed to act after receiving numerous notices from Louis Vuitton that certain websites that it hosted in China were selling products that infringed on Louis Vuitton's trademarks.

It appears that if you know about the infringement, are encouraging the infringement, or fail to act after receiving notice of the infringement, you have the potential for liability for user-generated content. What this means for website owners is that if they are notified of trademark infringement, they should promptly remove the infringing material. It is not a bad idea to include a takedown procedure for trademark infringement similar to that for copyright infringement in your terms of use and to obtain insurance covering these risks. See also question 5.5 (Can a Company be vicariously liable for the posts of an employee?) and question 1.6 (Can I be sued for defamatory items posted on my blog or website by others?).

8.5 DOES MY WEBSITE HAVE TO BE ACCESSIBLE TO PEOPLE WITH DISABILITIES?

In 1990, the Americans with Disabilities Act (ADA), 42 U.S.C. 12182, was passed in an attempt to level the playing field, so to speak, for those with disabilities. Since approximately 20 percent of our population has a disability,[247] the law makes sense. It essentially "prohibits discrimination on the basis of disability in employment, programs and services provided by state and local governments, goods and services provided by private companies, and in commercial facilities."[248]

The United States Justice Department has indicated that the ADA does apply to the Internet: "Covered entities under the ADA are required to provide effective communication, regardless of whether they generally communicate through print media, audio media, or computerized media such as the Internet. Covered entities that use the Internet for communications regarding their programs, goods, or services must be prepared to offer those communications through accessible means as well."[249] A covered entity is an employer with fifteen or more employees. In addition, a business that serves the public is considered a public accommodation. If the business that serves the public has a website, you would assume that it will need to provide effective communications to the public that uses that website through accessible means.[250]

In *National Federation of the Blind, et al. v Target Corporation*,[251] Target was sued because its retail website, Target.com, was not accessible to the blind in violation of the ADA. Although the organization's motion for a mandatory injunction to require Target to make its site accessible was denied, the court made it clear that the Federation could proceed with its lawsuit. Target agreed to settle by paying $6 million to the Federation and agreeing to modify its website with the input of the Federation. Although this case was decided in California and may not set a national precedent, it does seem consistent with the Justice Department's previous position. The Department of Justice website notes that it is currently seeking to update its ADA standards to require websites to be accessible.[252]

Even if you are not legally required to have an accessible website, it is a good business practice. One way in which to make your website accessible is by using universal design. This has the advantage of being accessible on a number of browsers. Without universal design, graphics or unusual fonts on your website will not display correctly on some handheld devices or old versions of browsers. In addition, if you use universal design and you are required to maintain an accessible website, you will not need a separate text-only site in order to comply.

8.6 WHAT IS OBSCENITY, AND DOES IT APPLY TO ME?

The legal standard for obscenity was defined in *Miller v. California*.[253] In deciding whether or not a particular item is obscene, and therefore not protected free speech, the court will consider: "(a) whether 'the average person, applying contemporary community standards' would find that the work, taken as a whole, appeals to the prurient interest . . . (b) whether the work depicts or describes, in a patently offensive way, sexual conduct specifically defined by the applicable state law; and (c) whether the work, taken as a whole, lacks serious literary, artistic, political, or scientific value."[254]

Both the states and federal government have laws regarding obscenity. It is easy to say that obscene material is not permitted on the Internet, but it is more difficult to decide in advance if a particular item is legally obscene. The *Miller* decision requires an analysis of community standards. Obviously, communities vary in their interests and tolerations. If you have any concerns at all about the materials you wish to make available on your website, you should seek an attorney's advice in advance regarding the legal requirements and limitations to which you will be subject.

It is important to note that the Communications Decency Act does not protect obscenity. This means that websites could be liable for user-generated obscenity or child pornography in certain circumstances. You are not protected as a website owner from liability from obscene materials posted on your website by third-party users. For this reason, you should make very sure that it is not possible for users to do this. It should be addressed not only in your terms of use, but also in your monitoring policies.

8.7 ARE CONTRACTS ENTERED INTO OVER THE INTERNET LEGAL?

Yes. Contracts can be formed through both electronic communication and websites. The ESIGN Act of 2000[255] provides that no contract can be declared illegal simply by virtue of its electronic form. Of course, all of the other elements of a contract must be present for a contract to be binding, whether the same is entered into online or otherwise. Some of the issues involved in one-sided agreements that appear on websites are discussed in Chapter 9. Remember, recent court decisions have found that if a website owner cannot show that a particular user has expressly agreed to its terms of use, they may not be binding.

8.8 DO I HAVE TO GIVE A WARRANTY FOR PRODUCTS I SELL OVER THE INTERNET?

There are two types of warranties that you need to concern yourself with: implied and express. An implied warranty results not from language that you provide to the consumer but from state law. An express warranty results from statements you make about products or services. It will probably not be possible under your state's laws to have your customers completely waive their warranty rights. The implied warranties of fitness and merchantability required in virtually every state with respect to the sales of goods cannot be waived. In many states, a reseller of goods is also liable for defective products. When you make a representation on your website about a specific product or service, these can be construed as express warranties. You want to make sure your representations comply not only with the FTC Endorsement Guides discussed in "Chapter 3," but also with FTC guidelines regarding warranties.[256]

You will want to be able to demonstrate the accuracy of statements made by you regarding products and services. If you cannot prove it, you probably should not say it. Under the FTC's Disclosure Rule, a written warranty must address five elements:

1. What does the warranty cover/not cover?
2. What is the period of coverage?
3. What will you do to correct problems?
4. How can the customer get warranty service?
5. How will state law affect your customer's rights under the warranty?[257]

In addition, there are federal and state laws concerning the language you do use if you decide to give your customers a written warranty. For example, "the Magnuson-Moss Warranty Act requires that every written warranty on a consumer product that costs more than $10 have a title that says the warranty is either 'full' or 'limited' [the Act calls these titles 'designations']. The title is intended to provide consumers, at a glance, with a key to some of the important terms and conditions of a warranty. The title 'full warranty' tells the consumers that the coverage meets the Act's standards for comprehensive warranty coverage. Similarly, the title 'limited warranty' alerts consumers that the coverage does not meet at least one of the Act's standards, and that the coverage is less than 'full' under the Act."[258]

Your best bet with respect to selling others' products or services is to make sure you understand their warranties and obtain a statement from them that they will protect you if you are sued for injuries caused by their products.[259] If you decide to give your customers a warranty based on your own products or services, make sure that the language in the warranty matches the statements on your website, your terms of use, and any contract that you require your customers to sign. You should also have an attorney review your warranty to make sure it complies with federal and state law.

8.9 DO I HAVE TO PAY TAXES ON PRODUCTS I SELL OVER THE INTERNET?

First, you will need to pay taxes on your income, even if you earn it over the Internet. Second, if you are selling goods over the Internet, you may need to collect sales taxes and remit them to the applicable state taxing authority. Essentially, a sales tax is a tax on the consumer collected by the seller and remitted to the state. A use tax is a tax on the consumer for products that he or she purchases that is remitted to the state by the consumer. Currently, forty-six states have use taxes that require individuals to report and pay them on 'untaxed' online purchases on their tax returns.[260] This means that those purchasing goods online are responsible for paying the tax directly to the taxing authority and that the online retailer does not need to collect it and remit it. This issue has become increasingly hostile as states scramble to tax everything they can to make up for their reckless spending and entitlement/ pension deficits.[261] The real issue is not that the online sellers are not collecting the tax, it is that the consumers are not paying the use tax and the states are not enforcing these laws. Regardless, it is important to understand what you as a seller are required to do.

The federal courts have found retailers to be liable to collect sales taxes for online sales in some circumstances but not in others. The rule, which has not been evenly applied, indicates that online retailers need only collect taxes from consumers in the states where the retailer also has a physical presence. However, in the case of *St. Tammany Parish Tax Collector v. Barnesandnoble. com LCC*,[262] the court held that despite the fact that Barnes & Noble had stores in Louisiana and sold online to customers in Louisiana, it did not have to collect sales taxes in Louisiana for its online sales. It reasoned that the products were delivered by common carriers and the stores were owned by a different subsidiary.

"Right now, Amazon collects sales taxes in only seven states. It's set to add seven more by 2016. According to the National Conference of State Legislatures, states that currently collect sales tax are Kansas, Kentucky, New York, North Dakota, Texas, Washington, and Pennsylvania. States that will collect in the future: New Jersey, Virginia, Indiana, Nevada, Tennessee, South Carolina, California."[263] What this means is that if you live in one of these states, you will probably need to be collecting sales taxes on your online sales. These laws change frequently. I would recommend that you speak with your accountant about your responsibilities with respect to your state and the states to which you sell.

8.10 AM I LIABLE FOR INFRINGING MATERIAL POSTED ON MY SITE BY SOMEONE ELSE?

Another issue arising in the area of copyright law is contributory infringement. Under this legal theory you could be found liable for infringing material that is posted onto your blog or website by others. There are several ways to protect yourself in this situation. First, you could disallow comments. Second, you could include an agreement on your site that requires posters to represent that they have the right to post the content. Third, you could monitor third-party posting and remove questionable material, provided your terms of use permit you to do this. Fourth, you may assert protection under the Digital Millennium Copyright Act if the blog or site can be considered an Internet service provider. This would require you to remove infringing content once notified of the infringement. These protection strategies are discussed more thoroughly in question 8.4 (Am I liable for what other people post on my site?).

8.11 AM I LIABLE IF SOMEONE STEALS INFORMATION FROM MY SITE?

First, if you are subject to the Gramm-Leach-Bliley Act (GLBA), you are required to provide certain protections in the area of financial privacy and safeguards for consumers' financial information. Those subject to GLBA include not only businesses that provide financial products and services to consumers, but also those involved in lending, brokering, or servicing consumer loans, preparing tax returns, and providing financial advice or credit counseling. These "financial institutions" are also regulated by the FTC.[264] If you are involved in marketing for these financial institutions, you are also subject to the GLBA. If you are one of the above types of financial businesses or a business that receives information from such businesses, you are subject to the GLBA, which requires that you develop standards relating "to administrative, technical, and physical safeguards:

1. to insure the security and confidentiality of customer records and information;

2. to protect against any anticipated threats or hazards to the security or integrity of such records; and

3. to protect against unauthorized access to or use of such records or information which could result in substantial harm or inconvenience to any customer."[265]

The GLBA Security Guidelines require that the covered entities "develop computer security programs, identify foreseeable risks to consumer information, and put in place measures to monitor and reduce the risk of such programs." There are other types of businesses that are subject to specific legislative privacy regulations, including those that deal with patients' medical records (i.e., health insurers, health care providers, and those who obtain records from these businesses) and those whose websites can be accessed by the residents of California. If you are in any of these health fields, then the Health Insurance Portability and Accountability Act (HIPAA) would apply to you. Similarly to the GLBA, there are privacy and safeguarding requirements.

If your website can be accessed by the residents of California, you will be subject to the Online Privacy Protection Act of 2003 Business and Professions Code Sections 22575–22579.[266] This was the first state law that required operators of commercial websites or online services that collect personal information on California residents through a website to conspicuously post a privacy policy on the site and to comply with its policy. The policy requires the website operator to (1) identify the personally identifiable information collected and with whom it is shared and (2) describe how it will notify users of its site of material changes to its privacy policy, among other things.[267] California law also requires notification to consumers of security breaches. See question 4.5 (Do states have privacy laws?) for more information.

Even if you are not covered by the GLBA, HIPAA, or the California Online Privacy Protection Act, there are still circumstances that could make you liable for the loss of customer information.[268] You have a common-law duty, and in many situations a statutory duty, to protect the confidential information that you collect on your website. Failure to take reasonable safeguards that results in damage to your users can lead to a claim of negligence or breach of statute.

In 2008, the FTC brought an action against Compgeeks.com,[269] the operator of the retail website Geeks.com, for "failing to provide reasonable security to protect sensitive customer data." The FTC indicated that it had the right to proceed under its statutory mandate to prevent deceptive and unfair trade practices. Although this case was settled, it established a strong precedent in this area as the FTC is the main enforcement body in these types of cases.

As is typical of many retail websites, Compgeeks.com collected information from consumers to obtain authorization for their credit card purchases (including their names, addresses, credit card numbers, etc.). In early 2008, hackers had entered the site and accessed this credit card information. The problem that the FTC had with Compgeeks.com was not that it collected the information, but that it stored it in unencrypted text on its computer network. The FTC also noted that Comgeeks.com did not employ any protections against hackers even though there were relatively inexpensive ways to do so. The proposed FTC settlement[270] prohibits Compgeeks.com from misrepresenting how it collects and protects a customer's private information and requires the company to implement and maintain "a comprehensive information security program that is reasonably designed to protect the security, confidentiality, and integrity of personal information collected from or about consumers."[271]

TJX was also investigated by the FTC in connection with a security breach.[272] According to the FTC complaint, a hacker was able to obtain information on "tens of millions of credit and debit payment cards that consumers used at TJX's stores, as well as the personal information of approximately 455,000 consumers who returned merchandise to the stores. Banks have claimed that tens of millions of dollars in fraudulent charges have been made on the cards and millions of cards have been cancelled and reissued."[273]

The complaint also alleged that TJX:

- Created an unnecessary risk to personal information by storing it on, and transmitting it between and within, its various computer networks in clear text;
- Did not use readily available security measures to limit wireless access to its networks, thereby allowing an intruder to connect wirelessly to its networks without authorization;

- Did not require network administrators and others to use strong passwords or to use different passwords to access different programs, computers, and networks;
- Failed to use readily available security measures, such as firewalls, to limit access among its computers and the Internet; and
- Failed to employ sufficient measures to detect and prevent unauthorized access to computer networks or to conduct security investigations, such as patching or updating antivirus software.[274]

The FTC settlement with TJX echoes the others we have read requiring TJX to implement a security plan and be subject to a security audit every two years for the next twenty years.[275]

See also question 4.8 (What happens if someone steals information from my website?).

8.12 HOW CAN I AVOID LIABILITY FOR SPAM?

Contrary to popular belief, spam is not illegal. Although there are some states with stricter laws, the federal CAN-SPAM Act (otherwise known as the Controlling the Assault of Non-Solicited Pornography and Marketing Act)[276] does not ban spam but prohibits false advertising and designates disclosure items, such as accurate subject lines in emails, opt-out procedures to allow recipients to stop receiving your emails, the labeling of commercial emails as advertisements or solicitations, and the addition of the sender's physical address in addition to their email address. Does this mean you can send out unsolicited emails? Yes, if you comply with the CAN-SPAM Act and applicable state laws (which is the difficult part of the equation).[277] Currently, California[278] and Delaware[279] are the only states that do not permit unsolicited emails. They only allow commercial emails when someone has signed up on a mailing list. Most other states, while not prohibiting commercial email, require that unsolicited emails contain the designation "advertisement" in the subject line and an opt-out mechanism in the body of the email. In addition to federal and state laws, your ISP provider's terms of use may also prohibit certain spamming activities. Most of the cases in which people have been sentenced to jail for spamming have involved not only a violation of these laws but also some type of fraudulent conduct as well (such as using fake return email addresses), sending emails in amounts which could crash a company's server or as part of a phishing scam.[280]

Your best bet when you send any type of mass email is to do it in reasonable amounts, use accurate subject line descriptions, include your email and physical address, provide an opt-out provision, and then make sure you take anyone off your mailing list who requests it. Remember: California and Delaware do not permit commercial mass emails unless the recipients have signed up on your mailing list.[281]

9 DOCUMENTS AND NOTICES
ON WEBSITES

In the case of *CollegeNet v. XAP*,[282] a court entered a judgment against XAP for violating its own privacy policy. Even though its privacy policy specifically indicated that personal data would not be shared with third parties without the users' express consent, XAP was found to have engaged in deceptive trade practices when the company sold its users' personal information regarding student loans and financial aid to financial institutions without first obtaining the users' consent. CollegeNet sued for damages (as this conduct affected its business) and was awarded $5.4 million. That is a big price to pay for not reading your own policy. The lesson here is that when you copy someone else's privacy policy and it does not match what you actually do, you could be found liable for damages. What XAP did was deceptive because it led its users to believe that the information they provided while using the site would be kept private. If you copy someone's privacy policy or draft one on your own that indicates that you do not share information when you actually do, you could be held liable under a number of legal theories.

There is a lot of confusion about what is required and what is not permitted on a website. As I discussed in my introduction, I have had clients tell me that they copied their privacy policy and terms and conditions from someone else's website having no real idea what they were representing to their users. If you do not know what your privacy policy even means, how can you possibly comply with it?

This chapter will clear up some of the confusion regarding privacy policies, terms of use, and disclaimers on websites. It provides details concerning which types of websites are required to have a privacy policy, what that policy should consist of, and some of the items that should not be included. It explains the penalties for failing to have a legally required privacy policy. Chapter 9 also demonstrates how terms of use can protect the reader, as well as its limitations. Finally, it explores disclaimers and how and when they can be used.

9.1 DO I NEED A PRIVACY POLICY?

It is commonly known that information placed on the Internet stays on the Internet. What many people are only beginning to realize is that their personal information is being sold to third-party networks or otherwise shared. Our information about our habits, identity, and the websites we visit is collected and disseminated almost continuously. Facebook's advertising revenues alone are $3.7 billion.[283]

There are a number of statutes that may require you to include a privacy policy on your website, including the Graham-Leach-Bliley Act (which applies to "financial institutions"), the Health Insurance Portability and Accountability Act (which applies to health care providers and others in the health care billing industry), the Children's Online Privacy Protection Act (which applies to websites that collect information from children under thirteen), and the California Online Privacy Protection Act (which applies to websites that collect information from residents of California).[284]

Because there are laws regarding the collection and dissemination of personal and business data as described earlier, it is important for any website that collects customers' or visitors' data to have a well-defined and easily accessible Internet privacy policy, including a notice of what data is being collected, a choice to opt-out of such collection, access to the data by the particular individual, and adequate security to prevent unauthorized misappropriation or dissemination of the data.

The FTC is primarily responsible for enforcing privacy regulations. In addition to having a well-defined privacy policy, you should also be able to enforce it. This requires you to stay up to date with the most current technology available to secure information as well as with the most current statutory and regulatory requirements.[285]

Your privacy policy should be placed in a prominent position on your website. Although many of my clients do not wish to display "legal jargon" on their homepages, at the very least you should provide the label "Privacy Policy" in contrasting letters with a tab or a link to the actual policy on the top of the landing page. Although not to have the policy on the landing page is understandable from an aesthetic and possibly a marketing standpoint, it is important to understand that if your privacy policy, terms of use, and disclaimers will not be seen by the users visiting your site, they have no value. If you are selling things on your website or collecting credit card information for any reason, you could have an action brought against you by the FTC for (1) failing to have a privacy policy, (2) failing to accurately define what you do with private information, and (3) failing to secure the data you collect.

9.2 WHAT HAPPENS IF I DO NOT HAVE A PRIVACY POLICY?

A privacy policy is important because it informs the users of your site what you are going to do with their information. It can certainly help you avoid liability under state and federal laws dealing with privacy issues.[286] If you do not have a privacy policy and you operate a type of business that is required to have one, you could be subject to an investigation by the FTC. If you are not required to have one but do in fact collect personal information, you could run afoul of state laws without even knowing it. It is good practice to post a privacy policy because it works as a contract between you and the user. If you do have a prominently displayed policy, users cannot claim they were unaware that you were providing their email address to your affiliates, etc.

9.3 WHAT SHOULD I INCLUDE IN A PRIVACY POLICY?

It goes without saying that there are different privacy requirements with respect to different industries. In addition, states also have privacy requirements. While it is impossible to provide suggestions that would apply to everyone, the following, at a minimum, should be included in your privacy policy:

- What information is being collected from your users and how you use it;
- With whom the information will be shared;
- Whether you use cookies and/or other tracking software;
- How users can gain access to and change the information they provide to your site;
- How users can stop information from being shared with third parties;
- How consumers will be notified of changes to the privacy policy; and
- What the effective date of the current version of the privacy policy is.

Your privacy policy needs to be "conspicuously posted" on your website. Although this is not a complete list of all privacy laws that may apply, there are additional requirements if (1) you are subject to the GLBA or HIPAA, (2) you have residents of California who access your website, or (3) your website caters to minors. If your site collects information from children under the age of thirteen, then you are bound by the Children's Online Privacy Protection Act.[287] It is a very good idea to indicate that if your business is sold, the information collected via the website will also be transferred to the new owners. Include a mechanism for users to acknowledge any changes to the privacy policy, such as an "I Accept" button. Finally, and I cannot overstate this enough, you must make sure that your privacy policy reflects what you actually do.

9.4 WHAT SHOULD NOT BE IN A PRIVACY POLICY?

Do not indicate that you will not collect information without the users' consent, if in fact you do collect it (and most of you will). Most commercial websites do collect IP addresses, email addresses, user configuration settings, and how the user arrived at the website through standard web server access logs. One mistake many of my clients make is simply copying a similar website's privacy notice on their own sites. In addition to possible copyright violations, the policy may indicate that you are collecting and/or distributing users' information contrary to your actual practice. It is safer to include a broad privacy policy that allows you to do more than you actually do than one that is more restrictive. In fact, it may be considered a deceptive trade practice if you later change the policy to permit additional uses of the users' information.

There are many statutes that regulate online privacy. As mentioned above, the Children's Online Privacy Protection Act (COPPA), which is enforced by the FTC, regulates the ability of websites to collect personal information from children under the age of thirteen. Failure to comply with COPPA can result in significant penalties. After an FTC investigation, Iconix Brand Group, Inc.[288] agreed to pay a $250,000 civil penalty because of its violations of COPPA. The FTC found that Iconix knowingly collected, used, or disclosed personal information from children on its website without first obtaining the parents' permission.

Iconix owned several apparel labels popular with children and teens. On its website, it required its users to provide personal information, including names, email addresses, zip codes, and in some cases mailing address, gender, and date of birth, in order to receive information about these brands and to enter sweepstakes. On its website, Mymuddworld.com, Iconix also had a forum which allowed girls to post stories and photos online. This activity was found by the FTC to violate COPPA because the parents were not given the opportunity to opt out of their children's sharing of information. Essentially, COPPA requires operators of websites targeting children under thirteen years of age (or that knowingly collect personal information from them) to obtain the parents' consent before collecting or disclosing any information from the underage users. These websites are also required to have an easy-to-understand privacy policy on their sites.

Because Iconix's privacy policy stated that it would not collect personal information from children without obtaining prior parental consent, contrary to its actual practice, it was found to have violated COPPA. In addition to the civil penalty, Iconix was required to delete all of its unlawfully collected information.[289]

9.5 DO I NEED TERMS OF USE?

If you have a website that is used by consumers or permits online posts, you should have terms of use. Terms of use (also known as terms of service or terms and conditions) set out the conditions under which your users agree to use your site. These terms should be prominently posted on your website and require the user to acknowledge reading and complying with them. One of the most important reasons to include terms of use on your website is the ability to claim immunity under the Digital Millennium Copyright Act (DMCA). The DMCA provides immunity to an Internet service provider and website owner with respect to posts made by third parties on the website which violate copyright laws. If you include a provision explaining how individuals can notify you when they believe something posted on your website violates their copyright (and otherwise comply with the act), you will be able to claim immunity from suit by the copyright owner.

To receive protection under the DMCA, you will need to comply with Section 512(c)(2) of the act, which includes posting a copyright policy on your website and designating an agent to receive notices of takedown notices. If you permit users to post comments or photos on your website and you do not register the agent with the US Copyright Office and pay the registration fee, you will not receive DMCA protection. The policy should be included in your terms of use or as a separate policy. It will help insulate you from liability for the posting of infringing materials by third parties. The following is the pertinent language in Section 512(c)(2):

> **(2) Designated agent.** — The limitations on liability established in this subsection apply to a service provider only if the service provider has designated an agent to receive notifications of claimed infringement described in paragraph (3), by making available through its service, including on its website in a location accessible to the public, and by providing to the Copyright Office, substantially the following information:
>
> **(A)** the name, address, phone number, and electronic mail address of the agent.
>
> **(B)** other contact information which the Register of Copyrights may deem appropriate.
>
> The Register of Copyrights shall maintain a current directory of agents available to the public for inspection, including through the Internet, in both electronic and hard copy formats, and may require payment of a fee by service providers to cover the costs of maintaining the directory.[290]

Aside from this important protection, the terms of use will act as a contract between you and your users. In order to be binding, the terms must be reasonable and agreed to by the user. This means you should include an "I Agree" button for your users to click indicating that they have read and agree to the terms. The terms of use will provide guidelines for what users can do on your website and the consequences for failing to comply. They will help to explain your privacy, copyright, and user policies. As with a privacy policy, you should not copy someone else's. First of all, that is copyright infringement. Second of all, the terms may not cover what your website needs. As with any contract, it is a good idea to get the input of an attorney.

9.6 WHAT HAPPENS IF I DO NOT HAVE TERMS OF USE?

Terms of use are the contract terms explaining what a user can and cannot do on your website. If you do not indicate that they are granting you a license to any of their posts and that you have the right to edit or change other people's posts, they may claim infringement by you (as your changes would be considered a derivative work). You want this right to allow you to remove or edit posts that may subject you to liability for copyright or trademark infringement as well as tort liability (defamation, trade libel, etc.).

In addition, if you do not have terms of use, you will not be able to claim protections under the Digital Millennium Copyright Act or the Communications Decency Act.

9.7 WHAT SHOULD I INCLUDE IN THE TERMS OF USE?

Generally, the following items should be contained in your terms of use:

- What can and cannot be posted by users
- Who can access your site and who cannot (children under the age of eighteen, residents of California, etc.)
- A disclaimer of liability for information posted or linked to the website
- A notice of your copyright and trademark ownership
- A request that anyone linking back to your website include a credit
- A provision allowing you to delete or modify user-generated content
- A provision indicating that anyone posting on your website is granting you a license to use his or her post
- A provision allowing you to terminate or restrict access to a user's account and to delete or modify any information posted on it
- A provision indicating that your state's laws apply to any disputes and where such disputes may be brought[291]
- Consequences for posting in violation of the terms
- Prohibitions against pornography, spamming, trademark or copyright infringement, defamation, flaming, etc.
- How the terms can be changed and how you will notify the users of the changes
- A provision allowing you to terminate someone's usage of your website for any or no reason at all

With respect to how you post your terms of use, there are two important aspects. First, the terms of use should be prominently displayed. Second, you should be able to prove that your users had notice of the terms of use by requiring them to click an "I Agree" button before they can access your website. While many websites just indicate that using the site constitutes agreement to the terms of use, some recent court cases have held that this is not enough to enforce your terms.

In the *In re Zappos.com Inc., Customer Data Security Breach Litigation*,[292] Zappos' terms of use were held to be unenforceable because Zappos could not show that the plaintiffs had consented to the terms of use requiring arbitration of any claims. This ruling came after a data security breach on the Zappos website affecting twenty-four million consumers. Some of those affected filed suit, and Zappos tried to have the cases dismissed because of the arbitration provision in its terms of use. The court found the terms of use themselves invalid because of the ability of Zappos to change them "at any time," rendering the "contract" illusory and thus unenforceable under contract law.

Similarly, in *Nguyen v. Barnes & Noble*,[293] the court denied Barnes & Noble's motion to compel arbitration as required in its terms of use after a lawsuit in federal court was filed against it because the plaintiff did not have "constructive notice" of the terms of use and Barnes & Noble was unable to show that Nguyen had agreed to same. Like in the Zappos case, the terms were on the website but were not prominently featured, nor was the customer (Nguyen) required to agree to them in connection with his online purchase.

It seems clear from these cases that indicating in your terms of use that anyone using your website is bound to them is simply not enough. You are required to show that your users agreed to be bound to the terms of use. Current best practices require you to have customers click on an "I Agree" button before they access your site and to require another affirmation of your terms as part of the checkout process if they are making purchases from your website.

9.8 CAN I CHANGE MY TERMS OF USE?

Even if your terms of use contains a provision that allows you to change the terms at any time, you probably will not be able to make significant changes that adversely affect your users unless you gain their consent to the new terms. Although some courts have held that a company is within its discretionary power to modify its terms under certain conditions,[294] the general rule of law is that you cannot modify a contract without new consideration. Obviously, if you are not paying the users (or otherwise giving them something of value) to permit you to modify your terms, there is no consideration. In addition, the act alone of changing terms unilaterally can be deemed unconscionable and thus unenforceable. As mentioned above in the *Zappos* case, the judge found the entire terms of use unenforceable because of the ability of the website owner to change its terms at any time.

Similarly, in the case of *Comb v. PayPal, Inc.*,[295] an arbitration clause which was added to PayPal's online terms of use at a later date without notice to the users of the website was declared invalid. Users of the PayPal site must click their agreement to PayPal's terms of use. In this case, the terms of use contained a provision indicating that they could be changed at any time without notice. When PayPal tried to add some pretty onerous language, the court found it to be unconscionable because it would put up enormous barriers to suit by its users who had already agreed to the original terms of use. I believe that if PayPal had permitted the users to opt out of the changes or required them to click their agreement to the new changes before continuing to use the site, the result may have been different.[296]

In general, in addition to having users consent to your terms of use, assuming you have a provision permitting you to make changes to the terms, make sure you obtain your users' consent to such terms before being able to continue to use the website.

9.9 WHAT IS A DISCLAIMER?

A disclaimer is a statement renouncing legal responsibility. It is used in all types of situations where a seller is trying to limit his or her exposure for liability. Generally, if you are a reseller, you would not want your liability to exceed the purchase price of the items sold, whereas manufacturers will be unable to limit their liability if someone is injured by a product that they designed and manufactured. What you can disclaim depends completely on the circumstances.

Although disclaimers can provide some protection, they are not uniformly enforced, because of the differences in state laws. If they are overused or overly broad, they may drive off users. They have been used in the past to indicate that web content may not be current, that the opinions on the applicable website are not those of the owners, that the website is not giving advice but providing information only, or that links are only provided as a courtesy and that the owner is not liable for the products, content, or privacy policies of such links. Always remember that even if you post a disclaimer on your blog or website, it will probably not show up in RSS (really simple syndication) feeds, because such feeds usually only show the most current post, not the entire site.

Although a court may find a disclaimer unenforceable, it is a good policy to include one to at least assert your position that you are not liable for incorrect information posted on your website, that you are not responsible for links from your website or their content, that you are not giving advice but merely providing the website as a source of general information, that you are not forging a relationship with any users of the site, etc. If you are in a litigious field such as law, medicine, or financial services, you will want an attorney to help you prepare your disclaimer.

9.10 IS A DISCLAIMER FOR THE INFORMATION I AM SHARING SUFFICIENT TO PROTECT ME FROM LIABILITY FOR WHAT I PUT ON MY WEBSITE OR BLOG?

You have probably noticed that many websites which provide information or advice often indicate that such information is provided on an "as is" basis. The idea behind these statements is that you want to prevent others from relying to their detriment on statements made on your website, especially those statements posted by others. If you include information yourself and do not update it, such information can become outdated and maybe even false. A disclaimer can limit your liability in these types of situations. So far, in the United States there has been very little case law to determine the validity of these website disclaimer statements.

Any time people may use information you provide on your website, it is a good idea to include a disclaimer, but do not expect it to completely resolve you of liability for everything on your website. You can still be held liable for false, misleading, or incorrect information. Generally, a disclaimer can be used to indicate that:

- You are providing general information, not advice specific to anyone's issue,
- Your website is not a substitute for obtaining medical care of legal advice (or whatever would be appropriate),
- You are not responsible for material contained in a linked website,
- You are not responsible for anything posted by users of your website or readers of your blog,
- You are not responsible for postings which are not up to date, and
- You are not responsible for errors or omissions on your website.

Even if you post these disclaimers, a court could find you liable anyway, especially for information that is inaccurate or not up to date. In order for a disclaimer to be valid, it must be agreed to. The court will look to see if it is conspicuously displayed on your website and whether the user gave his or her consent to the terms of the disclaimer. It would be very helpful to have a page that requires the users to agree to your terms of use (which would contain your disclaimer and privacy policy) before they could access your site. You should also conspicuously post your disclaimer where it cannot be missed on your website, display it in all capitals, and keep it brief. In any case, a reference to your terms of use should be prominently located on your first page and should contain at the very least an "I Agree" button.

9.11 WILL A DISCLAIMER PROTECT ME FROM INACCURATE STATEMENTS ON MY WEBSITE?

Although I could not find any recent US cases protecting a defendant based on a website disclaimer, in 2010 a California court held that a disclaimer by Facebook regarding "click fraud" did not protect Facebook against lawsuits. In the case of *In re Facebook PPC Advertising Litigation*,[297] several Facebook advertisers brought a class action against Facebook because they had been charged for fraudulent clicks. Facebook tried to have the suit dismissed because of its disclaimer, which stated:

> I . . . UNDERSTAND THAT THIRD PARTIES MAY GENERATE IMPRESSIONS, CLICKS, OR OTHER ACTIONS AFFECTING THE COST OF THE ADVERTISING FOR FRAUDULENT OR IMPROPER PURPOSES, AND I ACCEPT THE RISK OF ANY SUCH IMPRESSIONS, CLICKS, OR OTHER ACTIONS. FACEBOOK SHALL HAVE NO RESPONSIBILITY OR LIABILITY TO ME IN CONNECTION WITH ANY THIRD-PARTY CLICK FRAUD OR OTHER IMPROPER ACTIONS THAT MAY OCCUR.

Although the court dismissed the claim as it related to "click fraud" performed by third parties, it allowed the claim for breach of contract to proceed because of Facebook's failure to prevent "invalid clicks," which the disclaimer did not specifically address.

There is also an interesting UK case addressing this issue. In the case of *Patchett v SPATA*,[298] although the court held that companies could be liable if they made inaccurate claims on their websites, the disclaimers used on their websites offered them sufficient protection in this case. The Swimming Pool and Allied Trades Association (SPATA) operated a website that referred consumers looking for a swimming pool contractor to its members. After using a contractor listed on the site, Patchett wound up suffering losses of £44,000 after the contractor went bankrupt. Patchett sued SPATA for negligently providing the reference to the contractor on its website and not clearly disclosing that this particular contractor was not covered by the SPATASHIELD warranty. The court held that the disclaimer on the website was sufficient notice to the Patchetts that they needed to do their own due diligence prior to hiring any of the contractors listed on the site. Because of the disclaimer, SPATA was found not liable for the Patchetts' damages.

Again, there are not many US cases involving the enforceability of website disclaimers. Disclaimers are used by businesses in order to limit their liability to their customers. When used on a website, they are intended to limit the website owner's liability to its users. As a general rule, disclaimers (like your privacy policy and terms of use) should be conspicuously displayed, highlighted in some way (such as contracting text or **BOLD CAPS**), and easy to understand.

9.12 WHEN WILL A DISCLAIMER NOT PROTECT ME?

You most likely will not be able to disclaim your intentional acts, negligence, breach of contract, infringement, most tortious conduct, personal injury, and statutory warranties. Valid disclaimers are generally limited in scope, i.e., they only renounce responsibility for specific items as opposed to a blanket disclaimer against "any and all losses, of any kind." Generally, a far-reaching statement is less likely to be enforced than a well-defined and limited statement. At a minimum, the disclaimer must be placed conspicuously on the website.

As mentioned earlier, my clients generally object to having a disclaimer on the first web page on their websites or requiring a user to click its acceptance before entering their sites, but this truly is the best location and the best policy.[299]

Overall, you may include the disclaimer and privacy policy in your terms of use, provided they are clearly labeled and the disclaimer is in all capital letters. You would want the terms of use easily accessed from your first page (i.e., a tab or button on the top of the page which directs users to the proper page). Of course, the best way to protect yourself would be to have the terms of use appear when someone tries to access your website and an "I Agree" button (requiring initials in a box), which must be pressed for the user to access the rest of your site.

9.13 IS THERE ANYTHING ELSE I SHOULD INCLUDE ON MY WEBSITE?

In addition to terms of use, a privacy policy, and a disclaimer, you should also consider the following depending on the purpose of your website and whether or not you permit user-generated content to be posted. First, you should make sure you understand the laws regarding torts, intellectual property, consumer fraud, advertising, and contracts. If you are in a specialized field (or doing marketing work for those in a specialized field), you should make sure you understand the statutes applicable to that field (such as the privacy requirements for medical and financial fields). You should review your website to make sure you are not using copyrighted or trademarked materials without consent. You should include takedown procedures in your terms of use for both tortious (such as defamation and obscenity) and intellectual property (such as copyright and trademark) alleged violations. To receive protection under the Digital Millennium Copyright Act, you must notify the Copyright Office of your designated agent to receive takedown notices. You must notify your employees and independent contractors of all of these things to prevent them from creating liability for you. You should also have written agreements with your employees and independent contractors holding them responsible for their violations of law, requiring them to keep your confidential information confidential, and setting who will own what after the relationship is over (such as Twitter handles and followers, Facebook pages and passwords, client lists, any content they create, etc.).

Another area of risk is security. If you operate a website, you must protect your users' personal information. This requires you to keep up with standard security measures, to encrypt certain information, and to not store confidential information on your computer longer than you need to. You should also actively seek to protect your intellectual property. As discussed earlier, make a list of your intellectual property, document your ownership, and do not permit others to use it without a written license agreement. As soon as you become aware of someone using your intellectual property, you must take action to stop that person or risk losing the right.

This book attempts to explain some of the most common laws with which you will need to comply, but it does not contain everything. You need to understand the laws of the states in which you do business in addition to understanding the federal statutes. Failure to do so can result in fines, lawsuits, and potential criminal penalties. You will most likely need an attorney to help you with this.

10 LEGAL CONSIDERATIONS
WHEN SETTING UP AN E-BUSINESS

In *Crabbe v. United States,*[300] the court upheld a thirty-seven-month jail sentence against Crabbe for failing to pay payroll taxes. Crabbe, who was a partner in a business, was found criminally responsible despite the fact that he was not the partner responsible for the day-to-day operation of the company, made efforts to correct the payroll tax filings, and eventually paid the back taxes. His partner's action led to the violation of the federal tax laws, but because he was part of a partnership, Crabbe was found guilty also.

This case demonstrates how sloppy bookkeeping, failure to outline each partner's responsibilities in writing, and not understanding the law can not only subject you to liability but also potentially land you in jail. This partner could have avoided this situation by becoming informed about the difference between a contractor and an employee and understanding his legal responsibility as a partner in this situation. General partnerships are probably the most risky form of business. In addition, because no formality is required, you may be operating as a partnership without even knowing it.

This chapter covers the factors to consider when forming a legal entity to house an e-business. It then explains the differences between e-business sites and informational or blogging sites in terms of risks for business debts and liabilities. After explaining the advantages and disadvantages of each type of entity, the chapter goes on to discuss the many federal, state, and local requirements applicable to setting up an Internet business. It spells out how to choose and register the name of the business, how to make the initial tax filings, and when to obtain an accountant and an attorney. Finally, it clarifies how to legally handle employees, what types of insurance are applicable to e-businesses and bloggers, and what tax issues can arise.

10.1 IF I HAVE AN INTERNET BUSINESS, DO I NEED TO INCORPORATE?

Even if you work from home, there are many laws with which you must comply. And while most people are familiar with the protections of incorporation, there are a number of ways to structure your business. Your choice will be affected by the number of owners, the extent of control you desire over the business, and your need to avoid the risk of your personal assets being subject to the debts of the business. One of the first places you can go to for information is www.sba. gov the Small Business Association website. It is extremely user-friendly and will help direct you to the laws and issues of which you should become aware. There are also Small Business Development Centers located at many college campuses that provide free or low cost assistance.

In terms of whether you should incorporate or not, you should become familiar with all of your options before making that decision. This chapter will discuss the main types of legal structures. If you start a business on your own without making any formal filings, you will be automatically considered a sole proprietor. Similarly, if you go into business with someone else without making any formal filings, you will automatically be considered to be in a general partnership. Both of these structures will subject your personal assets to the debts of the business.

10.2 DO BLOGGERS NEED TO INCORPORATE?

If you are providing a purely informational blog, you will probably not need to incorporate. However, if your blog is related to your business or you plan on using your blog at some point to generate income, you may want to consider the advantages and disadvantages of the various entities discussed in this chapter. Regardless of whether you are selling anything on your blog or not, there are certain risks involved in blogging that could subject you to liability as discussed in earlier chapters. Setting up a corporation, LLC, or other limited liability vehicle will not protect you against a lawsuit for actions that you took personally. For example, although incorporating will provide you protection against business debts of the corporation, it does not protect you against tort liability, such as a claim of defamation. I recommend that bloggers (or other entities that post their opinions or report news online) obtain media insurance, which is discussed in question 1.5 (Don't anti-SLAPP laws protect me?).

10.3 WHAT IS A SOLE PROPRIETORSHIP?

If you will be operating your business on your own, desire to make all of the business decisions, and are not concerned with your liability for the debts of the business, you will most likely operate as a sole proprietor. The risk associated with this type of structure is that you could be personally liable if you have business debts above the assets and income of the business or liability beyond your insurance. With the sole proprietor form of legal structure, your personal assets and income are subject to the debts and liabilities of your business. If you do not register as any other legal entity, and you are operating on your own, you will be considered a sole proprietorship. A sole proprietorship is the easiest form of ownership because you essentially are the business. You simply report your business income on Schedule C for your federal income tax return. If you will be operating your business as a sole proprietor but will be using a business name other than your own, you will need to register your business name.[301]

Federal Tax Forms for Sole Proprietorships

- Form 1040: Individual Income Tax Return
- Schedule C: Profit or Loss from Business (or Schedule C-EZ)
- Schedule SE: Self-Employment Tax
- Form 1040-ES: Estimated Tax for Individuals
- Form 4562: Depreciation and Amortization
- Form 8829: Expenses for Business Use of Your Home
- Employment Tax Forms[302]

Advantages of a Sole Proprietorship

- It is the easiest and least expensive way to set up your business.
- You make all of the business decisions yourself.
- There are minimal legal restrictions.
- You are entitled to all of the income generated by the business.
- The profits from the business are reported on the owner's personal tax return.
- The business is easy to dissolve.

Disadvantages of a Sole Proprietorship

- Sole proprietors are personally responsible for all of the debts against the business.

- Their personal assets can be reached to pay business debts.
- The business will dissolve upon your death and is difficult to sell.
- It is more difficult to obtain financing for your business.
- You may lose certain tax deductions that you could have had otherwise had you incorporated (i.e., medical insurance deductions are treated differently).

10.4 WHAT IS A PARTNERSHIP?

If you will be doing business with one or more people, you will be considered a partnership by default. When Molly came to my office, she indicated that she was going to be selling her jewelry online through a website she created. It was not until thirty minutes into her description of the business that I understood that her sister made the jewelry and would be involved in the business. Because of the introduction of a second person, Molly's business shifted from a sole proprietorship to a partnership. After determining that Molly and her sister were not concerned about potential liability (and were insured for the same), we explored how they wanted the business to work. Generally, all profits, liabilities, and debts of the partnership are shared equally by the partners. Like a sole proprietorship, the partners make all of their own decisions and report business income on each partner's personal federal tax return.) Although there is an informational return that must be filed, there is no federal partnership tax. Similar to a sole proprietorship, if you have business debts above the assets and income of the business or liability beyond your insurance, the partners will be personally liable. Also like a sole proprietorship, a partnership can be formed by default when no other business election is made.[303] Because Molly and her sister did have some concerns about Molly's desire to form other businesses and the time to which she would be able to devote to the jewelry business, I suggested that they write up a partnership agreement that spelled out what would happen if Molly (or her sister, for that matter) wanted out. A partnership agreement can spell out all of the legal duties and responsibilities of each of the partners, how the profits would be shared, how disputes would be resolved (this is an especially tricky issue when you have an even number of partners), and how a partner can leave the partnership. The agreement can also indicate how much money each partner will contribute to the start-up of the business. In the case of Molly and her sister, Molly provided the start-up costs, while her sister provided an equal amount in completed jewelry and jewelry supplies. It was expected that Molly would be responsible for the online end, while her sister focused on making the product. They planned on splitting the profits equally after being reimbursed for any out-of-pocket costs.

Federal Tax Forms for Partnerships

- Form 1065: Return of Partnership Income
- Form 1065 K-1: Partner's Share of Income, Deductions, Credits
- Form 4562: Depreciation and Amortization
- Form 1040: Individual Income Tax Return
- Schedule E: Supplemental Income and Loss
- Schedule SE: Self-Employment Tax
- Form 1040-ES: Estimated Tax for Individuals
- Employment Tax Forms[304]

Advantages of a Partnership

- It is easy to set up.
- It has minimal legal constraints.
- It is easier to raise funds for it than for a sole proprietorship.
- The profits from the business are reported directly on the partners' personal tax returns.
- You can join efforts with someone who has skills in the areas in which you do not.

Disadvantages of a Partnership

- Partners are jointly and severally liable for the actions of the other partners and the debts of the business.
- Each partner's personal assets may be reached for business debts and liabilities.
- You must file an informational tax return (unlike a sole proprietor).
- Disagreements are hard to resolve when an even number of partners are involved.
- You may lose certain tax deductions that you would otherwise have had if you had incorporated (i.e., medical insurance deductions are treated differently).
- The business could end upon the withdrawal or death of a partner.

Like with sole proprietorship, if you do not designate the type of legal entity, and you are working with one or more people, you will be automatically considered a general partnership. In a general partnership all of the partners share responsibility for management decisions, liabilities, and profit or loss. Unless you have a written agreement to the contrary, equal shares of the profit and loss are assumed.

10.5 WHAT IS A CORPORATION?

A corporation is the most complex type of entity and is subject to more regulations than a sole proprietorship or general partnership, but affords you limited liability.[305] Limited liability means that your personal assets are protected from the debts of the corporation in most circumstances because the corporation is considered a separate legal entity. Corporations can be formed by an individual or a group by filing Articles of Incorporation in the state in which you desire to incorporate.[306] A corporation is owned by its shareholders and is managed by a board of directors.[307] The shareholders, board of directors, and officers generally are not personally liable for the debts or liabilities of the corporation.[308]

A corporation must file its own income tax return each year. In some situations this can result in double taxation because the corporation first pays taxes on the income of the corporation and then again if the shareholders receive dividends or the officers (who are also shareholders) receive a salary. This double taxation can be avoided by filing for S corporation status within the time indicated in the statute.[309] A corporation, unlike a sole proprietorship, generally has a perpetual life. In other words, if a sole proprietor were to die, his or her business would no longer exist. If a shareholder dies, the business still exists under the structure of the corporation. A corporation can hold title in its own name, be sued in its own name, and enter into contracts in its own name. This is probably the most important advantage as you are able to protect your personal assets from these potential debts and liabilities in most situations. The corporation is owned by its shareholders. If you are choosing to incorporate, please see an accountant so that you completely understand the tax ramifications of doing so. In addition, if there will be more than one shareholder, you may want to consult an attorney to draft a shareholder agreement to cover situations similar to those discussed in question 10.4 (What is a partnership?).

Federal Tax Forms for Corporations

- Form 1120 or 1120-A: Corporation Income Tax Return
- Form 1120-W: Estimated Tax for Corporations
- Form 4625: Depreciation
- Employment Tax Forms
- Other forms as needed for capital gains, sale of assets, alternative minimum tax, etc.[310]

Advantages of a Corporation

- The shareholders are not generally responsible for the corporation's debts or liabilities.
- It is a separate legal entity from the shareholders.
- You can sue in the name of the corporation.
- It is easy to transfer the assets of the corporation (sell the corporation).
- A corporation does not dissolve upon the death of a shareholder (continuity of existence).
- Corporations can raise capital through the sale of its stock.
- A corporation is entitled to certain tax deductions not permitted to sole proprietorships and partnerships.

Disadvantages of a Corporation

- Setting up a corporation involves more time, money, and formality than other forms of organization.
- Corporations are subject to more regulations than sole proprietorships.
- Corporations require continual maintenance in order to maintain the limited liability aspect (must follow corporate formalities).
- Incorporating may result in double taxation because the corporation is taxed first and then the shareholders and officers could be taxed again under certain circumstances.[311]

10.6 WHAT IS A SUBCHAPTER S CORPORATION?

If you meet the requirements of the IRS, you may elect to become a subchapter S corporation. This election allows shareholders to pass the profits of the business through to their personal tax returns and avoid double taxation.

Corporations can elect S corporation status by filing Form 2553 with the IRS. The form must be signed by all of the shareholders on a timely basis. In addition, the corporation must be domestic, have no more than 100 share-holders, and have only one class of stock. Because of the specificity of these requirements, I would recommend consulting an accountant before filing your incorporation papers.

Federal Tax Forms for Subchapter S Corporations

- Form 2553: Subchapter S Election
- Form 1120S: Income Tax Return for S Corporation
- From 1120S K-1: Shareholder's Share of Income, Deductions, Credits
- Form 4625: Depreciation
- Employment Tax Forms
- Form 1040: Individual Income Tax Return
- Schedule E: Supplemental Income and Loss
- Schedule SE: Self-Employment Tax
- Form 1040-ES: Estimated Tax for Individuals
- Other forms as needed for capital gains, sale of assets, alternative minimum tax, etc.[312]

Advantages of a Subchapter S Corporation

- It has the same advantages as a C corporation.
- It has no corporate taxes (profits are passed through to shareholders).

Disadvantages of a Subchapter S Corporation

- Limitations exist on the type and number of shareholders you can have.
- Profits can only be allocated per the stock allocation.
- Many additional requirements exist per the tax code.
- You cannot pass business debt through to shareholders; the same poli-cy applies to limited liability company members.

10.7 WHAT IS A LIMITED LIABILITY COMPANY?

A limited liability company (LLC) is owned by "members" who either manage the business themselves or chose a manager on their behalf. As with the other entities, you are required to comply with the laws of the state in which you organize.[313] The advantage to an LLC is that it allows the members to be sheltered from personal liability, like the shareholders in a corporation, but does not require a separate tax return like a corporation. The profits and debts are treated more like in an S corporation or partnership.[314] An LLC is usually required to have an operating agreement that spells out, among other things, how members can transfer their interest. This document is of sufficient complexity to require the input of an attorney. Like a corporation or partnership, if you have more than one member, you will want to spell out what happens if one member wants to sell his or her membership interest. Because the federal government does not recognize LLCs for taxation purposes, you will need to file a Form 8832 to classify your LLC as a corporation for tax purposes. If no election is made, a multimember LLC will be taxed as a partnership and a single-member LLC will be taxed as a sole proprietorship.

Federal Tax Forms for LLCs

- Form 8832: Entity Classification Election
- Form 1040: Individual Income Tax Return
- Schedule C: Profit or Loss from Business (or Schedule C-EZ)
- Schedule SE: Self-Employment Tax
- Form 1040-ES: Estimated Tax for Individuals
- Form 4562: Depreciation and Amortization
- Form 8829: Expenses for Business Use of Your Home
- Form 1065: Return of Partnership Income
- Form 1065 K-1: Partner's Share of Income, Deductions, Credit
- Employment Tax Forms
- Form 1120S: Income Tax Return for S Corporation
- Form 1120S K-1: Shareholder's Share of Income, Deductions, Credits
- Form 4625: Depreciation
- Employment Tax Forms
- Schedule E: Supplemental Income and Loss
- Other forms as needed for capital gains, sale of assets, alternative minimum tax, etc.[315]

Advantages of an LLC

- The members are not generally responsible for the debts of the corporation.
- It is a separate legal entity from the members.
- You can sue in the name of the LLC.

- An LLC does not dissolve upon the death of a member (continuity of existence).
- You can choose how to be taxed.
- Single-member LLC reports taxes on Schedule C.
- Multimember LLC reports taxes on either partnership or corporate returns.
- Profits and losses can be shared as indicated in the operating agreement (which does not have to match ownership interests).
- It can pass business debts to members.

Disadvantages of an LLC

- Filing and annual fees are usually higher than those of corporations.
- Each state's LLC laws are different (less consistency than with corporations).
- Each state's tax laws with respect to LLCs are different.
- If you convert an existing business, such as a corporation, into an LLC, there may be unintended tax consequences.
- The amount of loss you can deduct may be limited because of your limited liability for LLC debts.
- Passive activity loss limitation may restrict the amount of loss you can deduct.

10.8 DOES BECOMING AN LLC PROTECT ME IF I AM GIVING OUT ADVICE?

While forming an LLC or corporation does protect your personal assets from the debts of the business, if you do not comply with the formalities involved in such organizations, this limited liability protection can be lost. You must fully and completely comply with all of the laws and regulations regarding that form of ownership, or else a claimant could "pierce" through and obtain a personal judgment against you. At a minimum you must file your annual report and keep your personal and business bank accounts separate.[316] However, if you are giving out advice, as opposed to information, you will need to determine what regulations are involved with your profession. Some professions, like that of a psychotherapist, require a professional license. You may also need or desire to carry malpractice insurance or some type of errors and omissions insurance. For example, many of my life-coaching clients do maintain insurance through their professional association.

10.9 DO I HAVE TO GET A LICENSE TO OPERATE AN IN-HOME INTERNET BUSINESS?

In you are engaging in one of the activities regulated by the federal government, you may need to obtain a federal license. Some of these activities are the importation and interstate transportation of animals, the sale of alcohol, and the sale of firearms. Although each jurisdiction is different, you may also need to get a business license from your state, county, or municipality. Lucky for us, the Small Business Administration has put together a website which can help you make this initial determination. If you go to http://www.sba.gov/category/navigation-structure/starting-managing-business/starting-business/choose-register-your-busi you will be able to enter your zip code, and the site will direct you to the appropriate governmental agencies. For example, if you were to type in the zip code 60189, you would be directed to a page that lists a number of steps to be accomplished but also has links to the City of Wheaton and County of DuPage websites, where you can learn about business licenses. In this particular case, the City of Wheaton only requires licenses for certain types of business, such as those selling tobacco. The county website also had specific businesses listed that require licenses, such as tobacco sales and liquor sales businesses. You will also want to check your local zoning laws and homeowners association rules to determine if there are restrictions on what you can do in your home.

If you are located in a jurisdiction that does require a business license, it could be a simple $50 certificate indicating your business name or an annual fee based on gross sales. You will want to check with the city's tax collector for more information. If you live in an unincorporated area, you would check with the county. In addition, certain licenses would be required if you have employees or are manufacturing goods.[317]

10.10 DO I NEED TO REGISTER MY BUSINESS NAME?

If you are a sole proprietor doing business under a name that is not your legal name or a partnership doing business under a name other than the name of the partners, it is referred to as an "assumed" or "fictitious" name. Generally, you are required to register this "assumed" or "fictitious" name under your state's Doing Business As (d/b/a) statute (the name of the statute will vary). Each state's laws are different. You may also need to register with the county in which you are located. If your name is Joe Gerace and you operate a restaurant called Gerace's, you will probably not need to register that name. On the other hand, if your restaurant is called The Italian Thespian, you will need to file a d/b/a in most states.

In general, when corporations, LLCs, or limited partnerships are doing business under their legal name, such name is considered registered when the Articles of Incorporation, Articles of Organization, or statements of limited partnerships are filed in your state's registration office.[318] However, if you are operating under a different name from your registered entity, you may need to file for a d/b/a with the state and/or county where the business is located, as described above. You can visit the "Business Name Registration (Doing Business As)" page at www.sba.gov for more information. Each state's requirements (and many times links) are listed. After determining whether you need to file with the state or the county, you will, in many jurisdictions, file a notice in the local newspaper with your new name. In some jurisdictions, you will file the state registration with the county clerk's office. In most states, the registration will last for five years. Please note that although applying for trademark registration of your business name is not legally required, there may be certain benefits in doing so. This issue is more fully discussed in question 6.4 (How do I protect my mark?). Since your Internet business and/or blog will most likely be operating on a nationwide basis, the fullest protection would be to file a trademark application for your name if you want to prevent anyone else from using it and have the full arsenal of defenses to stop any infringement.

10.11 DO I NEED A TAX ID/EMPLOYER IDENTIFICATION NUMBER?

A federal tax identification number (otherwise known as an EIN) is used by the government to identify a business entity regardless of the type of organization. It will allow you to pay employees and independent contractors but is used for other purposes as well. By filing the IRS SS-4 form (which can now be done electronically, by fax, over the phone, or by mail), you will receive your EIN. If you apply over the phone or Internet, you can usually get your number immediately. The number is 800-829-4933. The online source is located at www.irs.gov/businesses/small/index.html. You will then need to contact your state's revenue agency for its version of the SS-4.[319] The IRS URL above has a link to each state's revenue department. You may need your EIN prior to registering your assumed name. Generally, regardless of your legal form, most banks will require an EIN for you to open a bank account in the name of your business so you might as well get one as soon as you decide on your form of legal entity.

10.12 DO I HAVE TO PAY TAXES?

In addition to making the filings in connection with your legal entity, name, and EIN, you may be required to pay taxes. This is handled at the federal, state, and local level and varies significantly from state to state. If you are engaged in a business or have formed a legal entity requiring the filing of a tax return, you will need to check with the IRS or your accountant regarding your federal filings. There are a number of state and local tax filings that you may need to make as well. You can check with the Small Business Administration (www.sba.gov/content/learn-about-your-state-and-local-tax-obligations) for more information. It has links for each state's tax department.

In most states, business owners are required to register their business with the state taxing authority. In addition to possible state income taxes, there could also be franchise taxes. The tax filings you will make will depend on the legal structure of your business. See the questions above regarding the tax requirements for the different entities.

Both the federal government and the states require certain employers to pay employment taxes. Depending on where you are located and where your employees are located, you may also need to pay for workers' compensation insurance and disability insurance.

Although the federal government does not require you to obtain a sales tax permit, most states do. In addition to business taxes required by the federal government, you will have to pay some state and local taxes. Each state and locality has its own tax laws.

If you will be collecting money from customers, you will most likely need to obtain a sales tax permit from your state or local government or possibly both. In some jurisdictions services are not taxed with a sales tax, but in others they are. If you sell products, you can receive a Sales Tax Exemption Certificate, which will allow you to avoid taxes on the purchase of the products you buy for resale. You will need to speak with your accountant regarding how you will pay taxes on the items or services sold. Each state varies significantly in its tax laws. You can become familiar with the issues by examining the Small Business and Self-Employment Tax Center page at www.irs.gov/Businesses/Small-Businesses-&-Self-Employed.

In Illinois, for example, it is recommended that before you make your first sale or hire your first employee, you register with the Illinois Department of Revenue. You will then receive a Certificate of Registration and Illinois Business Tax number (this is your state "tax" identification number or IBT number). You should also check with your county and local governments for any additional tax registrations that you will need to make.

10.13 DO I NEED AN ACCOUNTANT?

One thing I always recommend to my clients is that they find a good trustworthy accountant before they start setting up their own businesses. You should get several recommendations and check their references. An accountant will help you with all of the required tax forms, setting up a bookkeeping system, and recommending the proper legal entity based on your situation. As mentioned in question 10.1 (If I have an Internet business, do I need to incorporate?), while a corporation may shield your personal assets from business debts, you could also be in a double-taxation scenario as you will pay both corporate taxes on the income to the corporation and then personal income taxes on the income to you. Additionally, you may need help in making sure that all of the initial tax registrations have been done correctly. An accountant will also help you make the continued tax filings on time.

10.14 DO I NEED BUSINESS INSURANCE?

There are a number of different types of insurance you should consider when you start your own business. State law may also require you to maintain insurance depending on your type of business. In addition to a reliable accountant, you will want to find a trustworthy insurance agent. I do not recommend that you switch around. If you find someone you can trust, do not look for a lower rate each year. By establishing a relationship with your agent, you will have an ally if a claim ever comes up. Property insurance will protect you against the loss of your business assets, such as your computer equipment, inventory, etc. If the amount of these assets is small, you may be able to get by with a rider on your homeowner's policy. Liability insurance will cover claims by other people. This depends completely on whether you are selling products, providing services, or giving advice. Business interruption insurance will cover your business expenses during the time of casualty.

If your office burns down, this insurance will cover your fixed expenses during the time your business is not operating. Key man insurance (a politically incorrect term) is often required if you are in business with more than one person and get financing. It pays the business a sum of money if an important member of the business becomes disabled or dies. Officer and director liability insurance protects the officers and directors of a corporation for claims against them personally.

You will want to examine your current business insurance to make sure it protects you with respect to your online activities. Speak frankly with your insurance agent about what it is that you do online. Although the United Kingdom already provides social media insurance, the United States insurance companies tend to exclude social media from their policies. The three main areas that you would want coverage for are torts, intellectual property, and security. Lloyds of London and a few other companies have insurance specifically covering materials and sales via websites, including security of credit card numbers and other important data. If you post on other sites frequently or are a blogger, you may also want to consider standard media insurance that will protect you against claims of defamation or breach of privacy. Although these policies are pricey now, I imagine the costs of these policies will decrease as the insurance pool grows.

10.15 DO I NEED AN ATTORNEY TO START A BUSINESS?

Starting a new business involves three situations that can greatly benefit from the advice of an attorney: (1) deciding how to organize your business, (2) assessing the impact of laws and regulations on your business, and (3) understanding and minimizing the risks associated with your business. As I indicated above, there may be situations unique to you that require certain permits, registrations, or other protections that I have not discussed here. This is especially true in the case of any type of manufacturing business or other business that requires more than the use of your computer at home. Many attorneys will meet with you for a free consultation. This is also the time to discuss which, if any, state or local filings you will need to make and how you want to organize your business. (Ideally, you can find an attorney and an accountant who have worked together in the past since you may need advice from both.)

If you have decided to incorporate or organize as an LLC, I do recommend having an attorney set that up for you and allowing him or her to serve as your registered agent. This will shift the burden of filing the annual report to your attorney and also save you the embarrassment of having a lawsuit served on you at home or work (the service would be at the attorney's office). In terms of minimizing risk, an attorney can also talk you through the myriad of scenarios of which you may not have thought. It is difficult to make a blanket prediction that you will need an attorney without knowing the specifics of your business. I would never tell anyone that he or she does not need an attorney. As mentioned earlier, I also recommend an attorney if you are going into business with someone else. You always want to establish up front how the profits will be allocated, how the debts will be divided in the case the business fails, and what will happen if one person wants out or a new person wants in.

I do believe that having your website reviewed by an attorney occasionally is a good practice. As the law continues to evolve, there will be more restrictions placed on use of the Internet and websites and blogs in general.

10.16 WHAT DO I DO IF I HAVE EMPLOYEES?

As the sample case in the beginning of this chapter illustrates, the hiring of employees brings a whole new level of risk into the picture.[320] It is not true that you can avoid this by hiring only independent contractors, because many states will audit you to make sure that your independent contractors are not really employees in disguise.[321] The www.sba.gov website[322] outlines ten steps to follow regarding tax issues, which I will outline here.

Step 1: Obtain an Employer Identification Number

In question 10.11 (Do I need a tax ID/employer identification number?), I recommend obtaining an EIN for your business as one of your first steps. This number will be needed before you hire any employees. The EIN is used for tax reporting purposes when you have employees. To obtain an EIN, you can apply online or contact the IRS directly.

Step 2: Set Up Records for Withholding Taxes

The IRS states that you must keep records of employment taxes for at least four years. It is a good idea anyway to keep complete records for your business not only for tax purposes but also to help you value your business in the event you want to obtain a loan or sell your business. These employment tax forms include the Federal Income Tax Withholding Form (W-4), which is filed with the IRS on or before the first date of employment; the Federal Wage and Tax Statement Form (W-2), which is filed with the IRS and the Social Security Administration on an annual basis, showing the wages and taxes of the employee; and your state's required forms if you are required to withhold state income taxes.

Step 3: Employee Eligibility Verification (Form I-9)

You must complete Form I-9 to confirm your employee's eligibility to work in the United States. You are to keep these completed forms on file for three years after the date of hire or one year after the date the employee's employment is terminated, whichever is later, in the event of an audit by the US Immigration and Customs Enforcement.

Step 4: Register with Your State's New Hire Reporting Program

The Personal Responsibility and Work Opportunity Reconciliation Act of 1996 requires all employers to report newly hired and rehired employees to a state directory within twenty days of their hire or rehire date.[323]

Step 5: Obtain Workers' Compensation Insurance

State Workers' Compensation statutes require employers to maintain Workers' Compensation Insurance on their employees. Each state's requirements are different.[324]

Step 6: Unemployment Insurance Tax Registration

State unemployment insurance statutes require employers to pay unemployment insurance taxes. Again, each state's laws vary.[325]

Step 7: Obtain Disability Insurance (If Required)

California, Hawaii, New Jersey, New York, Puerto Rico, and Rhode Island require employers to obtain short-term disability insurance.[326]

Step 8: Post Required Notices

State and federal laws require employers to put up posters regarding employees' rights and employer responsibilities under various labor laws.[327]

Step 9: File Your Taxes

You will need to file quarterly (or more frequent) tax returns concerning your employees. I would recommend finding an experienced accountant to assist with these filings as the penalties for mistakes are so great.

Step 10: Get Organized, and Keep Yourself Informed

In addition to all of the tax and reporting requirements, it is a good idea to keep these files organized and accessible. Besides finding a good accountant, you may wish to hire a bookkeeper to assist you if this is not your strong suit.

CONCLUSION

Social media marketing is not a trend. I cannot even say it is where marketing is heading: It is where marketing is now. Regardless of your level of involvement with social media, there are legal risks involved. Whether you have a website of your own or post elsewhere, you need to have at least a basic understanding of intellectual property law, tort law, and the regulations that apply to the Internet. In this guide I have tried to cover the issues most relevant to you in these areas. There are two main obstacles to staying current with Internet law: (1) Each country, state, and federal government has its own set of laws and (2) many laws were written before the Internet and are being applied in unanticipated ways. Even the regulations written a year ago can become obsolete overnight as technology advances in ways not anticipated by the legislature.

As discussed earlier, anyone who posts on the Internet is an author and is subject to all of the same laws and regulations to which anyone else who publishes text is subject. There is a risk of tort liability for defaming someone and for copyright infringement if you copy someone's work. Neither the Communications Decency Act[328] nor the Digital Millennium Copyright Act[329] would protect you from liability for your own posts. They are designed to shield you in certain situations from liability because of the posts of third parties.

To avoid liability, you should obtain permission to use someone else's work, credit your sources, seek a release when you are going to mention or post a photograph of someone who is not a public figure or otherwise newsworthy on your site, avoid revealing private information about anyone, and do not make statements that you have not independently verified to be true.

Because of the potential for vicarious liability, if you have people working for you, you need to make sure they comply with your rules as well as the regulations that apply to your activities. You should also utilize written agreements regarding ownership of your work. Remember, when you hire an independent contractor to create any content or graphics for you, that person owns what he or she creates unless you have a written agreement stating otherwise. The same goes for your website designer.

Another area in which you want to utilize written agreements is on your website. It is becoming more important to have terms of use that your users consent to with an "I Agree" button, as more and more courts are requiring this. You should also spell out what your users can and cannot do on your site. You should prohibit profanity, flaming, copyright infringement, defamation, etc. You should specifically permit retweets, links to your site with proper attribution, the ability to forward articles that you create with proper attribution, and any other activities that you would like to encourage. You do not lose your ownership rights if you expressly tell people how they can use your work, but you will always want those who link to or forward your materials to include your information. I've seen some permissions that require a link to one's homepage as well.

One of the areas that I am concerned about is potential federal regulation of the Internet. So far we have been able to prevent some of these insidious laws (such as the Protect Intellectual Property Act and the Stop Online Piracy Act, which were halted in 2012 due to incredible public derision).[330] However, there are some federal regulations that may need to change, such as the exorbitant fines being levied under the Copyright Act against people who download a song from the Internet. Because the MPAA and RIAA have such a strong lobby in Washington, unless the public becomes more vocal about the fairness of forcing college students to pay thousands of dollars in fines for downloading a $0.99 song "illegally," nothing will be done.

Internet law is in a constant state of flux. It is impossible to state what the law is today, because it varies from jurisdiction to jurisdiction and the laws on the books are outdated by the time they go to press. Technology changes that quickly. I predict that the following issues will be debated and potentially legislated in the near future:

- The excessive statutory damages being awarded in copyright infringement cases

- The inability to fully monitor trademarks due to the Internet
- Mobile apps
- Geo-locating
- SLAPP suits and enforcement fallout
- Cyberbullying
- Cyber-impersonation
- Copyright infringement and fan art
- Social media ownership after death[331]

I sincerely hope that this guide has been of use to you and that you will continue to reference it as issues arise in your use of social media. Social media is an amazing way to reach people and gauge conversations. We are only just beginning to tap its uses. It is not difficult to imagine a time when six degrees of separation no longer exists—that you will have a way to reach anyone at any time. As we trade privacy rights for the ability to connect, we are also creating a new world in which those who wish to live completely off the grid will have to give up their digital identity. Those who embrace social media will assist in developing new techniques for people to collaborate and in ways of which we are just beginning to dream. I for one am excited to be on the forefront of this digital and social revolution. I hope we connect soon.

ENDNOTES

INTRODUCTION

1   Read more at www.nydailynews.com/entertainment/gossip/disgruntled-ex-miss-usa-contestant-ordered-pay-organization-5m-article-1.1223305#ixzz2Gw1uSZes and at www.huffingtonpost.com/2012/12/31/beauty-queen-sheena-monnin-shocked-trump_n_2387906.html

2   David Goldman, "Tweet costs Mark Cuban $50,000," *CNNMoneyTech*, January 9, 2013, at http://money.cnn.com/2013/01/09/technology/social/mark-cuban-tweet-fine/index.html?iid=s_mpm

3   Ibid.

4   See http://blog.hubspot.com/blog/tabid/6307/bid/8594/Social-Media-Marketing-By-The-Numbers-Infographic.aspx

5   This figure is based on research by BIA/Kelsey—a marketing forecast firm retrieved from http://www.marketingprofs.com/charts/2012/9567/us-social-media-ad-spend-to-reach-92b-in-2016

6   http://mashable.com/category/social-media-marketing/

CHAPTER 1

7   139 Cal.App.4th 1423 (Cal.App. 2006).

8   *Obsidian Finance Group, LLC v. Cox*, 812 F.Supp.2d 1220 (2011).

9   In *Gertz v. Robert Welch, Inc.*, 418 US 323 (1974), the court held that although states are free to establish their own standards of liability in defamation cases, if the standard is less than actual malice, then only actual damages may be awarded. This means that there usually has to be some showing of harm to the plaintiff.

10   *New York Times v. Sullivan*, 376 US 254 (1964).

11   The First Amendment protects statements of opinion against claims of defamation. See *Milkovich v. Lorain Journal Co.*, 497 US 1 (1990).

12   *Colt v. Freedom Communications, Inc.*, 109 Cal.App.4th 1551 (2003).

13   Electronic Frontier Foundation, *Online Defamation Law* (2012). Retrieved from www.eff.org/issues/bloggers/legal/liability/defamation

14   Restatement (Second) of Torts, Section 583.

15   *Armstrong v. Shirvell*, No. 2:11-CV-11921, 2012 US Dist. LEXIS 65697 (E.D. Mich. May 10, 2012); see also Kevin Dolak, "Attorney Andrew Shirvell Ordered to Pay 4.5 Million for Attacks on Gay Student," *ABC News*, August 17, 2012, at http://abcnews.go.com/US/attorney-andrew-shirvell-ordered-pay-45-million-attacks/story?id=17028621#.UOXKD3cWy_M

16   Libel per se includes allegations of criminal conduct, contagious diseases, impotence, lack of virginity, or lack of professional qualifications. Libel per se permits private individuals and public figures to bring a claim without having to prove damages.

17   514 US 334 (1995).

18   78 Pa. D&C 4th 328 (2004).

19   09 L 5636 (Cook County, Ill., 2009).

20   The description of this lawsuit was taken from the blog www.intheeyesofthelaw.com, authored by Kimberly A. Houser.

21   See 47 U.S.C. Section 203, et al.

22   See question 9.7 regarding terms of use.

23   See the website for the anti-SLAPP Resource Center on information about what to do if served with a SLAPP suit at www.thefirstamendment.org/antislappresourcecenter.html

24   40 Cal.4th 33, 146 P.3d 510 (Cal. 2006).

25   CCP § 425.16.

26   See Restatement (Second) of Torts § 578.

27   See 47 U.S.C. § 230.

28   See 489 F.3d 921 (9th Cir. 2007).

29   *Mazur v. eBay Inc.*, No. C 07-03967 MHP, 2008 WL 618988 (N.D. Cal. March 4, 2008); *NPS LLC v. StubHub, Inc.*, 25 Mass.L.Rptr. 478, 2009 WL 995483 (Mass. Super. Ct. Jan. 26, 2009); *Hy Cite Corp. v. badbusinessbureau.com*, 418 F. Supp. 2d 1142 (D. Ariz. 2005).

30   See Restatement (Second) of Torts § 652E.

CHAPTER 2

31   *Disney Enterprises, Inc. v. Showstash.com*, CV 07-4510 (D.C. Cal., 2008).

32   A work is considered to be in the public domain if (1) the copyright has expired, (2) the copyright has been abandoned or specifically

made available to the public, or (3) it has been created by the federal government.

33   See 18 U.S.C. § 2319(c)(1) and 17 U.S.C. § 506(a)(2). Prior to the enactment of this amendment to the Copyright Act, it was not illegal to download materials from the Internet for your own use. See www.justice.gov/opa/pr/1999/August/371crm.htm for the first prosecution under the NET Act.

34   Barbara M. Waxer and Marsha L. Baum, *Copyright on the Internet* (Boston, Mass.: Cengage Learning, 2007), 35.

35   See *Intellectual Reserve, Inc. v. Utah Lighthouse Ministry, Inc.* (D.C. Utah, 1999) and *MPAA v. pullmylink.com.*

36   No. 3:06-CV-276-L, 2007 WL 79311 (N.D. Tex. Jan. 9, 2007).

37   The Associated Press (AP) has been actively enforcing its copyrights ownership of news articles against those copying them online. Most news services pay a licensing fee to the AP to republish the AP news articles. Most recently, the AP filed suit against Meltwater, a news aggregator, alleging that it violated AP's copyrights by republishing its articles to Meltwater's subscribers without paying AP's license fee. See *Associated Press v. Meltwater US Holdings, Inc., et al.*, No. 12 Civ. 1087 (S.D.N.Y.), filed February 14, 2012.

38   17 U.S.C. §105. "Subject matter of copyright: United States Government works: Copyright protection under this title is not available for any work of the United States Government, but the United States Government is not precluded from receiving and holding copyrights transferred to it by assignment, bequest, or otherwise." United States Government work is defined in 17 U.S.C. § 101 — "Definitions: A 'work of the United States Government' is a work prepared by an officer or employee of the United States Government as part of that person's official duties."

39   17 U.S.C. § 403: "Notice of copyright: Publications incorporating United States Government works - Sections 401(d) and 402(d) shall not apply to a work published in copies or phonorecords consisting predominantly of one or more works of the United States Government unless the notice of copyright appearing on the published copies or phonorecords to which a defendant in the copyright infringement suit had access includes a statement identifying, either affirmatively or negatively, those portions of the copies or phonorecords embodying any work or works protected under this title."

40   www.youtube.com/static?gl=US&template=terms (June 9, 2010).

41   www.facebook.com/legal/terms (December 11, 2012).

42   Because the music is not being used for commercial purposes and certainly will not affect sales (except possibly in a positive way), there should be an exception carved out for background music. See question 2.1 (Can I copy information from other websites if I list them as sources?).

43   See question 7.7 (What can I do if someone infringes on my domain name?).

44   The Anticybersquatting Consumer Protection Act, 15 U.S.C. § 1125(d), holds people who register domain names that are confusingly similar to trademarks, doing so with a bad faith intent to profit from the marks, liable for damages.

45   2008 WL 760196 (Civil No. 06-526, N.D. Ga. March 21, 2008).

46   See the *Public Participation Project* website for links to the differing state anti-SLAPP laws at www.anti-slapp.org/your-states-free-speech-protection/

47   California Code of Civil Procedure § 425.16.

48   *Lenz v. Universal Music Corp.*, 572 F. Supp. 2d 1150, 1151-52 (N.D. Cal. 2008).

49   www.govtrack.us/congress/bills/112/s3493

50   In the case of *Bridgeport v. Combs*, 507 F.2d 470 (6th Cir. 2007), Sean Combs failed to respond to a cease-and-desist letter claiming copyright infringement, which resulted in a punitive damage award (which was later reduced) and a compensatory damage award of approximately $850,000 in statutory and compensatory damages.

51   See 18 U.S.C. § 2319.

52   757 F. Supp. 1046, 1049 (D. Neb. 1991).

53   134 F.2d 533, 535 (2d Cir. 1943).

54   For a list of these activities and the case sites, see the IT Law Wiki at http://itlaw.wikia.com/wiki/Willfulness

55   www.opencongress.org/bill/110-s3325/show

56   15 U.S.C. § 7701, et seq.

57   15 U.S.C. § 7704(a)(1).

58   584 F.3d 1240 (9th Cir. 2009).

59   Interestingly, Virginia's antispam law (Va. Code Ann. § 18.2-152.3:1) was declared unconstitutional by the Virginia Supreme Court.

Although it contains different language than the CAN-SPAM Act, the court's action serves as a reminder of how each jurisdiction treats Internet law differently. Jeremy Jaynes was found guilty of violating Virginia's law in 2004. His conviction was overturned because the court indicated that the criminal statute violated the First Amendment's protection of anonymous free speech. See *Jaynes v. Commonwealth of Virginia*, Supreme Court of Virginia, September 12, 2008, No. 062388. Note that while this decision does not have any impact on the federal CAN-SPAM Act, it does raise interesting constitutional law issues.

60   Case No. CV-10-4712-JF (N.D. Cal. March 28, 2011).

CHAPTER 3

61   The text of the Endorsement Guides can be found on the FTC website at www.ftc.gov/os/2009/10/091005revisedendorsementguides.pdf

62   FTC File No. 102 3055.

63   See question 1.6 (Can I be sued for defamatory items posted on my blog or website by others?) with respect to defamation and other civil torts.

64   False advertising occurs when you make false or misleading statements about your own product or service. Trade libel occurs when you make false or misleading statements about someone else's products or services.

65   2012 WL 252846, Case No. 11-C-1103 (E.D. Wis. 2012).

66   16 CFR Part 255.

67   See *Hanberry v. Hearst Corp.*, 276 Cal.App.2d 680 (1969).

68   15 U.S.C. 7701 et. seq.

69   FTC Endorsement Guides, 74 Fed. Reg. 53,124, 53,125 (Oct. 15, 2009) (codified at 16 C.F.R. pt. 255) at 53, 139 (example 5).

70   § 255.1(d) example 5 of the FTC Endorsement Guides.

71   See question 1.6 (Can I be sued for defamatory items posted on my blog or website by others?) with respect to defamation and other civil torts.

72   False advertising occurs when you make false or misleading statements about your own product or service. Trade libel occurs when you make false or misleading statements about someone else's products or services.

73   See question 1.6 (Can I be sued for defamatory items posted on my blog or website by others?) and question 3.3 (How do the new FTC Endorsement Guides affect those posting content online?) for more information on false advertising and trade libel.

74   The guides are administrative interpretations of the law intended to help advertisers comply with the Federal Trade Commission Act; they are not binding laws themselves.

75   Similarly, if a company refers to the findings of a research organization study that was paid for by the company, the advertisement must disclose the connection between the advertiser and the research organization. Likewise, if an employee recommends a product or service on a discussion board or blog, the employee is required to disclose that he or she is employed by the manufacturer or supplier of the service.

76   See Ian Paul, "Instagram reverses service terms: Is it good for users?," *PC World*, December 21, 2012, at www.pcworld.com/article/2022924/instagram-reverses-service-terms-is-it-good-for-users.html

77   841 So.2d 561 (Fla. Dist. Ct. App. 2003).

78   2010 WL 2767984 (Tex. App. Ct. 2010).

79   No. C 11-03474 MEJ. (N.D. Cal. 2012). This case is pending.

80   See Anne Fisher, "Who owns your twitter followers, you or your employer?" *CNN Money*, December 13, 2012, at http://management.fortune.cnn.com/tag/phonedog-v-kravitz/

81   In some jurisdictions, any expenditure of effort on the part of an entrant would satisfy the consideration element. In other words, requiring entrants to give something other than money could make your sweepstakes a lottery in some states.

82   Both Florida and New York require promotions in which the prize is over $5,000 to be registered. See NY Gen. Bus. Law 369 and FL Stat. 849.094.

83   www.dca.ca.gov/publications/legal_guides/u-3.shtml

84   See Facebook's terms of use. For more information on Facebook promotions, see Genevieve Lachance, "Facebook Promotions Know the Rules," *Social Media Today*, May 21, 2012 at http://socialmediatoday.com/node/512417

85   Twitter's rules are located at http://help.twitter.com/entries/68877-guidelines-for-contests-on-twitter. YouTube's terms are located at www.youtube.com/t/terms

86   15 U.S.C. 45(n).

87   15 U.S.C. 43(a).

88   *Doctor's Assocs., Inc. v. QIP Holders, LLC*, 2010 WL 669870 (D. Conn. Feb. 19, 2010).

89   See Sheila Shayon, "The Landmark Facebook Ruling That 'Rocked' Diageo," August 7, 2012, at www.brandchannel.com/home/post/2012/08/07/Facebook-Australia-Smirnoff-Ruling.aspx

90   *International Shoe Co. v. Washington*, 326 US 310 (1945).

91   130 F.3d 414 (9th Cir. 1997).

92   952 F.Supp. 1119, 1121 (W.D. Pa. 1997).

93   See Chapter 10 on important documents to include on your website.

94   See Michael Ratner, "Julian Assange is right to fear US prosecution," *UK Guardian*, August 2, 2012, at www.guardian.co.uk/commentisfree/2012/aug/02/julian-assange-right-fear-prosecution

95   HCA 56; 210 CLR 575; 194 ALR 433; 77 ALJR 255 (Australian High Court Opinion 2002).

96   www.abc.net.au/news/2004-11-12/dow-jones-settles-gutnick-action/584404

CHAPTER 4

97   www.hhs.gov/news/press/2011pres/02/20110222a.html

98   Fair Credit Reporting Act as amended by the Fair and Accurate Credit Transactions Act (FCRA/FACTA) (15 U.S.C.A. § 1681 et seq.); the Telephone Consumer Protection Act (TCPA) (47 U.S.C.A. § 227); the Driver's Privacy Protection Act (DPPA) (18 U.S.C.A. §§ 2721–25); the Electronic Communications Privacy Act (ECPA) (18 U.S.C.A. §§ 2510–22); and the Video Privacy Protection Act (VPPA) (18 U.S.C.A. § 2710).

99   42 U.S.C. §§ 1320 et. seq., HIPAA Privacy Rule, 45 CFR subtitle A, subchapter C, parts 160 and 164.

100   www.healthit.gov/providers-professionals/your-mobile-device-and-health-information-privacy-and-security

101   www.healthit.gov/providers-professionals/how-can-you-protect-and-secure-health-information-when-using-mobile-device

102   www.hhs.gov/news/press/2013pres/01/20130102a.html

103   15 U.S.C. Sections 6501, et seq.

104   See FTC 2012 report "Mobile Apps for Kids: Disclosures Still Not Making the Grade."

105   "The survey results show that, despite these generous parameters, a significant number of apps transmitted information from the device without disclosing this sharing to users. Indeed, while 59% (235) of the apps transmitted device ID, geolocation, or phone number either to the developer or a third party, only 20% (81) of the apps reviewed provided any privacy disclosures to users. The results also show that most of the data that was transmitted was sent to ad networks, analytics companies, or other third parties. Specifically, 56% (223) of the kids' apps reviewed sent the data to third parties, but only 20% (44) of these apps provided any privacy disclosures." FTC 2012 report "Mobile Apps for Kids: Disclosures Still Not Making the Grade," page 6.

106   See "FTC Strengthens Kids' Privacy, Gives Parents Greater Control Over Their Information By Amending Children's Online Privacy Protection Rule," at www.ftc.gov/opa/2012/12/coppa.shtm.

107   See "FTC Strengthens Kids' Privacy, Gives Parents Greater Control Over Their Information By Amending Children's Online Privacy Protection Rule," at www.ftc.gov/opa/2012/12/coppa.shtm

108   15 U.S.C. §§ 6801–6827.

109   Generally, such information can only be shared with affiliates of the financial institution and only with those affiliates having signed agreements with the financial institution stating that the affiliate will not resell or otherwise improperly utilize the customer information.

110   http://business.ftc.gov/documents/bus53-brief-financial-privacy-requirements-gramm-leach-bliley-act

111   As discussed in Chapter 9 regarding disclosures, this will not completely protect you, but it will help.

112   See question 8.1 (Is it safer to set up my own site or post on others' sites?).

113   Cal. Bus. & Prof. Code §§ 22575–22579 (2006).

114   See State Privacy Regulations, AICPA (2012) at www.aicpa.org/InterestAreas/InformationTechnology/Resources/Privacy/FederalStateandOtherProfessionalRegulations/StatePrivacyRegulations/Pages/default.aspx

115   www.ncsl.org/issues-research/telecom/security-breach-notification-laws.aspx

116 Cal. Civ. Code 1798.82 and 1798.29.

117 Cal. Civ. Code § 1798.82(a). Any person or entity that maintains computerized data that includes "personal information" that the person or entity does not own must notify the owner or licensee of that information about any such incident; Cal. Civ. Code § 1798.82(b). "Personal information" is defined as an individual's first name or first initial and last name in combination with any one or more of the following data elements, when either the name or the data elements are not encrypted: (1) Social Security number; (2) driver's license number or California identification card number; (3) account number or credit or debit card number, in combination with any required security code, access code, or password that would permit access to an individual's financial account; (4) medical information; or (5) health insurance information; Cal. Civ. Code § 1798.82(e).

118 Tom Kemp, "Buckle up with Cybersecurity. . . It's the Law," *Forbes*, February 1, 2012, at www.forbes.com/sites/tomkemp/2012/02/01/buckle-up-with-cybersecurity-its-the-law/

119 www.revisor.mn.gov/statutes/?id=325E.61&year=2007

120 www.leg.state.nv.us/NRS/NRS-603A.html

121 18 U.S.C. § 1030.

122 www.ftc.gov/opa/2012/12/epic.shtm

123 See Complaint, *In the Matter of Geocities*, No. C-3850 (FTC 1999), available at www.ftc.gov/os/1999/02/9823015cmp.htm

124 Complaint, Google, Inc., FTC File No. 102 3136 (Mar. 30, 2011).

125 www.ftc.gov/opa/2011/03/google.shtm

126 www.ftc.gov/os/caselist/0923093/110311twitterdo.pdf

127 www.ftc.gov/opa/2012/08/facebook.shtm

128 www.ftc.gov/os/caselist/0423160/050616comp0423160.pdf

129 No. 11-13694 (11th Cir. Sep. 5, 2012).

130 18 U.S.C. § 1030(a).

131 www.bakerlaw.com/files/Uploads/Documents/Data%20Breach%20documents/Data_Breach_Charts.pdf

132 47 U.S.C.A. § 227.

133 Case No. C10-1139-JCC (W.D. Wash. 2012).

134 www.nytimes.com/2012/04/08/technology/text-message-spam-difficult-to-stop-is-a-growing-menace.html?_r=0

135 www.whitehouse.gov/the-press-office/2012/02/23/we-can-t-wait-obama-administration-unveils-blueprint-privacy-bill-rights

136   www.ftc.gov/os/2012/03/120326privacyreport.pdf

137   "To address concerns about undue burdens on small businesses, the final framework [FTC recommendations in the Report] does not apply to companies that collect only non-sensitive data from fewer than 5,000 consumers a year, provided they do not share the data with third parties"; at www.ftc.gov/os/2012/03/120326privacyreport.pdf, page 10.

138   *In the Matter of Upromise, Inc.*, FTC File No. 102 3116 (Jan. 18, 2012) (proposed consent order), available at www.ftc.gov/os/caselist/1023116/index.shtm; *In the Matter of ACRAnet, Inc.*, FTC Docket No. C-4331(Aug. 17, 2011) (consent order), available at http://ftc.gov/os/caselist/0923088/index.shtm; *In the Matter of Fajilan & Assocs., Inc.*, FTC Docket No. C-4332 (Aug. 17, 2011) (consent order), available at http://ftc.gov/os/caselist/0923089/index.shtm; *In the Matter of SettlementOne Credit Corp.*, FTC Docket No. C-4330 (Aug. 17, 2011) (consent order), available at http://ftc.gov/os/caselist/0823208/index.shtm; *In the Matter of Lookout Servs., Inc.*, FTC Docket No. C-4326 (June 15, 2011) (consent order), available at www.ftc.gov/os/caselist/102376/index.shtm; *In the Matter of Ceridian Corp.*, FTC Docket No. C-4325 (June 8, 2011) (consent order), available at www.ftc.gov/os/caselist/1023160/index.shtm; *In the Matter of Twitter, Inc.*, FTC Docket No. C-4316 (Mar. 11, 2011) (consent order), available at www.ftc.gov/os/caselist/0923093/index.shtm

The above resource was cited in the March 2012 FTC privacy report at www.hldataprotection.com/uploads/file/FTC%20PrivacyReport_FINAL.pdf?&lang=en_us&output=json

139   See PCI Security Standards Council, *PCI SSC Data Security Standards Overview*, available at www.pcisecuritystandards.org/security_standards/ SANS Institute, *Information Security Policy Templates*, available at www.sans.org/security-resources/policies/ BITS, *Financial Services Roundtable BITS Publications*, available at www.bits.org/publications/index.php

See also, e.g., Better Business Bureau, *Security & Privacy—Made Simpler: Manageable Guidelines to help You Protect Your Customers' Security & Privacy from Identity Theft & Fraud*, available at www.bbb.org/us/storage/16/documents/SecurityPrivacyMadeSimpler.pdf

National Cyber Security Alliance, *For Business*, available at www.staysafeonline.org/for-business (guidance for small and midsize businesses).

Direct Marketing Association, *Information Security: Safeguarding Personal Data in Your Care* (May 2005), available at www.the-dma. org/privacy/InfoSecData.pdf

Messaging Anti-Abuse Working Group & Anti-Phishing Working Group, *Anti-Phishing Best Practices for ISPs and Mailbox Providers* (July 2006), available at www.antiphishing.org/reports/bestpractices-forisps.pdf, as cited in the March 2012 FTC privacy report.

140   *In the Matter of Google Inc.*, FTC Docket No. C-4336 (Oct. 13, 2011) (consent order), available at www.ftc.gov/os/caselist/ 1023136/index. shtm

141   http://ftc.gov/opa/2012/03/rockyou.shtm

142   www.ftc.gov/opa/2010/06/twitter.shtm

143   www.ftc.gov/opa/2010/06/twitter.shtm

CHAPTER 5

144   http://www.nlrb.gov/news-outreach/news-releases/settlement-reached-case-involving-discharge-facebook-comments

145   www.nlrb.gov/search/simple/all/facebook

146   29 U.S.C. §§ 151-169.

147   NLRB Case No. 34-CA-012576.

148   NLRB Case No. 13-CA-046452, 358 NLRB No. 164.

149   In another union case involving posts made on Facebook, the court affirmed the dismissal of a teacher in New Jersey. *In the Matter of the Tenure Hearing of Jennifer O'Brien, State-Operated School District of the City of Paterson, Passaic County,* #544-11 (OAL Decision: http://www.state.nj.us/education/legal/commissioner/2011/dec/544-11.pdf).

After becoming fed up with the behavioral issues of her first-grade students, she posted, "I'm not a teacher—I'm a warden for future criminals!" on her Facebook page. After receiving parent complaints, the teacher was fired by the school district. Although the teacher did have a First Amendment right of free speech, the court found that the post undermined the relationship between the school and the parents of the students. Again, because the post did not directly reference her dissatisfaction with how the school board was handling the issues related to the classroom but instead was critical about her students, the court felt the school was within its rights to terminate her.

150 Katherine, M. Scott, "When Is Employee Blogging Protected by Section 7 of the NLRA?" *Duke Law and Technology Review*, 2006, available at http://scholarship.law.duke.edu/cgi/viewcontent.cgi?article=1163&context=dltr

151 Lauren K. Neal, "The Virtual Water Cooler and the NLRB: Concerted Activity in the Age of Facebook," 69 Wash. & Lee L. Rev. 1715 (2012), available at http://scholarlycommons.law.wlu.edu/wlulr/vol69/iss3/8

152 For another excellent article examining Facebook postings and the NLRB, see Robert Sprague, "Facebook Meets the NLRB: Employee Online Communications and Unfair Labor Practices," *University of Pennsylvania Journal of Business Law* 14, no. 4 (2012), 957–1011.

153 www.aclu-md.org/press_room/64

154 www.ncsl.org/issues-research/telecom/employer-access-to-social-media-passwords.aspx

155 Michigan Internet Privacy Protection Act (PA 478), 2012.

156 Civil Case No. 06-5754 (FSH) (NJ DC 2009), not for publication

157 15 U.S.C. § 1681 et seq.

158 www.facebook.com/note.php?note_id=326598317390057

159 In *Smyth v. Pillsbury Co.*, 914 F.Supp. 97 (E.D. Pa. 1996), the court found that the company did not invade the employee's privacy by reviewing his emails.

160 15 U.S.C. § 1681 et seq.

161 "Two states, Connecticut and Delaware, require employers to give notice to employees prior to monitoring e-mail communications or Internet access. Colorado and Tennessee require states and other public entities to adopt a policy related to monitoring of public employees' e-mail"; Connecticut Gen. Stat.§ 31-48d and Del. Code § 19-7-705. See www.ncsl.org/issues-research/telecom/state-laws-related-to-internet-privacy.aspx.

162 http://digitalcommons.ilr.cornell.edu/cgi/viewcontent.cgi?article=1056&context=condec

163 Tamar Lewin, "Chevron Settles Sexual Harassment Charges," *The New York Times*, February 22, 1995, at www.nytimes.com/1995/02/22/us/chevron-settles-sexual-harassment-charges.html

164 www.ncsl.org/documents/employ/off-dutyconductdiscrimination.pdf

165 Minn. Stat. Ann. § 181.938.

166 "Twenty-nine states and the District of Columbia have enacted statutes giving some protections to employees who smoke. (See, Cal. Labor Code §§ 96(k), 98.6 (California); Colo. Rev. Stat § 24-34-402.5 (Colorado); Conn. Gen. Stat. § 31-40s (Connecticut); D.C. Code § 7-1703.03 (District of Columbia); 820 Ill. Comp. Stat. 55/5 (Illinois); Ind. Code § 22-5-4 (Indiana); Ky. Rev. Stat. Ann. § 344.040 (Kentucky); La. Rev. Stat. Ann. § 23:966 (Louisiana); Me. Rev. Stat. tit. 26, § 597 (Maine); Minn. Stat. § 181.938 (Minnesota); Miss. Code Ann. § 71-7-33 (Mississippi); Mo. Rev. Stat. § 290.145 (Missouri); Mont. Code Ann. §§ 39-2-313, 39-2-314 (Montana); Nev. Rev. Stat. § 613.333 (Nevada); N.H. Rev. Stat. Ann. § 275:37-a (New Hampshire); N.J. Stat. Ann. § 34:6B (New Jersey); N.M. Stat. Ann. § 50-11-3 (New Mexico); N.Y. Lab. Law § 201-d (New York); N.C. Gen. Stat. § 95-28.2 (North Carolina); N.D. Cent. Code §§ 14-02.4 (North Dakota); Okla. Stat. tit. 40, § 500 (Oklahoma); Or. Rev. Stat. §§ 659A.315, 659A.885 (Oregon); R.I. Gen. Laws § 23-20.10-14 (Rhode Island); S.C. Code Ann. § 41-1-85 (South Carolina); S.D. Codified Laws § 60-4-11 (South Dakota); Tenn. Code Ann. § 50-1-304 (Tennessee); Va. Code Ann. § 2.2-2902 (Virginia); W. Va. Code § 21-3-19 (West Virginia); Wis. Stat. § 111.31 (Wisconsin); Wyo. Stat. Ann. § 27-9 (Wyoming).)" See http://www.lungusa2.org/slati/appendixf.php

167 www.ncsl.org/issues-research/telecom/computer-hacking-and-unauthorized-access-laws.aspx

168 "An employer is subject to liability for torts committed by employees while acting within the scope of their employment." REST 3d AGEN § 2.04.

169 772 F. Supp. 2d 967 (N.D. Ill. 2011).

170 http://scholar.google.com/scholar_case?case=16227806786911947872&hl=en&as_sdt=2&as_vis=1&oi=scholarr

171 http://scholar.google.com/scholar_case?case=11711660463998513349&hl=en&as_sdt=2&as_vis=1&oi=scholarr

172 29 U.S.C. §§ 151-169.

173 18 U.S.C. § 2701 et seq.

174 15 U.S.C. § 1681 et seq.

175 15 U.S.C. § 1051-1127.

176   See *ETW Corp. v. Jireh Pub., Inc.*, 332 F.3d 915, 925-26 (6th Cir. 2003).

177   15 U.S.C. § 1681 et seq.

178   "Common law" is defined in part by *Black's Law Dictionary* (9th ed. 2009) as the body of law derived from judicial decisions rather than from statutes or constitutions. People often refer to common law as "judge-made law." Common law involves taking the holding in one case and applying the rationale for the decision to another. When judges do this, the courts are viewed as treating people who are involved in similar disputes in the same manner. This concept of following precedent (prior decisions) is called *stare decisis. Stare decisis* in Latin means "to stand by things decided."

When discussing cases in this legal guide, I have used them as examples of what could happen. You should know that when a court decision is made in one case, the new "law" only applies to future cases in that jurisdiction. What this means is that if I tell you about a case in California and your issue centers around your website in Illinois with respect to clients in Illinois, that California case is not precedent. It is, however, instructive.

CHAPTER 6

179   No. H-08-0337 (S.D. Texas 2008).

180   See www.uspto.gov

181   Common-law rights are those given to people or entities by judges' rulings in court decisions as opposed to the rights given by statutes. See www.uspto.gov/web/menu/statetmoffices.html for links to each state's trademark office.

182   See www.uspto.gov for more information on the trademark process.

183   This is one of the areas of law that I believe will be changing because of the difficulty in monitoring the entire Internet.

184   See 15 U.S.C. Ch. 22.

185   Wimberley is the name of a town near Austin, Texas.

186   For a while, the trademark office was not registering blog names. The original reason for excluding them was their failure to identify a product or service in commerce. Today it seems that the USPTO is more open to accepting such names for registration.

187 People are permitted to use your trademark without your consent for "fair uses," such as teaching, reporting, comment, criticism, and parody. Fair use is explained in question 2.1 (Can I copy information from other websites if I list them as sources?).

188 See question 10.10 (Do I need to register my business name?).

189 The rule is different for "famous marks." If you use someone's famous mark for your business, you may be "diluting" that person's or entity's rights. See question 7.7 (What can I do if someone infringes on my domain name?).

190 *University of Southern California v. University of South Carolina*, No. 1064 (D.C.S.C. 2009).

191 Lanham Act 15 U.S.C. § 1051 et seq.

192 *Internet Specialties West, Inc. v Milon-DiGiorgio Enters. Inc.* 559 F3d 985 (9th Cir 2009).

193 See 15 U.S.C. § 1125(d).

194 See Chapter 7 for information on steps to take when you discover infringement.

195 See 17 U.S.C. § 102.

196 See question 2.1 (Can I copy information from other websites if I list them as sources?).

197 See 17 U.S.C. § 106.

198 According to the US Copyright Office, "the term of copyright for a particular work depends on several factors, including whether it has been published, and, if so, the date of first publication. As a general rule, for works created after January 1, 1978, copyright protection lasts for the life of the author plus an additional 70 years. For an anonymous work, a pseudonymous work, or a work made for hire, the copyright endures for a term of 95 years from the year of its first publication or a term of 120 years from the year of its creation, whichever expires first. For works first published prior to 1978, the term will vary depending on several factors. To determine the length of copyright protection for a particular work, consult Chapter 3 of the Copyright Act (title 17 of the *United States Code*). More information on the term of copyright can be found in Circular 15a, *Duration of Copyright*, and Circular 1, *Copyright Basics*"; www.copyright.gov/help/faq/faq-duration.html. Also see Sections 302 and 305 of the Copyright Act.

199 See 17 U.S.C. § 504(c).

200 See the US Copyright Office's Circular #66: *Copyright Registration for Online Works* at www.copyright.gov/circs/circ66.pdf

201 What some have done is register their websites separately from any blog component. The blog component is then registered as a serial work. This, however, has not been proven in court to be a valid copyright registration as of this time and requires registration every three months.

202 See US Copyright Office's Circular #14: *Copyright Registration for Derivative Works* at www.copyright.gov/circs/circ14.pdf

203 See US Copyright Office's Circular #66: *Copyright Registration for Online Works* at www.copyright.gov/circs/circ66.pdf

204 188 F.Supp.2d 398 (S.D.N.Y. Feb. 28, 2002).

205 www.internetlibrary.com/pdf/Getaped-Shelly-Cangemi-SD-NY.pdf

206 See US Copyright Office's Circular #1: *Copyright Basics* at www.copyright.gov/circs/circ01.pdf

207 See www.copyright.gov/eco for more information

208 This could be months after you file but is faster than if you mail in your forms.

209 www.copyright.gov/eco/faq.html#eCO_1.3

210 See question 6.13 (Can I register my website with the Copyright Office?).

211 See US Customs and Border Protection website at https://apps.cbp.gov/e-recordations/.

212 *CLS Bank Intern. v. Alice Corp. Pty. Ltd.*, 685 F. 3d 1341 - Court of Appeals, Federal Circuit 2012 is a split decision which is expected to be reviewed by the Supreme Court.

CHAPTER 7

213 188 F.Supp.2d 398 (S.D.N.Y. Feb. 28, 2002).

214 www.internetlibrary.com/pdf/Getaped-Shelly-Cangemi-SD-NY.pdf

215 Read about the Jammie Thomas-Rassett case at http://news.cnet.com/8300-5_3-0.html?keyword=jammie+thomas-rasset. Also see question 2.14 (What do I do if I get sued?).

216 478 F. Supp. 2d 1240 (W.D. Wash. 2007) www.internetlibrary.com/pdf/blue%20nile.pdf.

217 See 17 U.S.C. § 512.

218 The following is an idea of what should be included in a takedown letter to an ISP provider:

- Your contact information
- Date the notice is being sent
- The ISP name and address/email

Include a subject line:

Notice of Copyright Infringement

Text of letter:

The copyrighted work at issue is the text/photo that appears on www.yourwebaddress.com/page X.

The offending work appears at www.infringingwebsaddress.com/page X.

It is my good faith belief that the use of the copyrighted materials described above is infringing on my copyright-protected material and is not authorized. I swear, under penalty of perjury, that the information in the notification is accurate and that I am the copyright owner or am authorized to act on behalf of the owner of an exclusive right that is allegedly infringed. By this letter, I ask that you remove the material under the authority of the Digital Millennium Copyright Act of 1998.

Sincerely,

Your Name

219   See 17 USC Section 504(b) and (c). Attorney fees are covered under 17 USC Section 505.
220   See 17 U.S.C. 504 (b).
221   17 U.S.C. § 512(c)(3)(B).
222   See 17 U.S.C. § 512(g)(2).
223   15 U.S.C. § 1125(d).
224   See 15 U.S.C. §§ 1051 et seq.
225   15 U.S.C. § 1125(a).
226   For a list of the state laws regarding trademarks, see www.uspto.gov/trademarks/process/State_Trademark_Links.jsp
227   *AMF, Inc. v. Sleekcraft Boats*, 599 F.2d 341, 348-349 (9th Cir. 1979).
228   *Sayeedi v. Walser*, 835 N.Y.2d 840 (2007).
229   In *Scarcella v. AOL*, the court found AOL's forum selection clause unenforceable under the facts in that case because although AOL indicated that all lawsuits against it had to be brought in Virginia, the court found the forum selection clause to be against public policy.

230   *Scarcella v. AOL*, 4 Misc. 3d 1024A (N.Y. Civ. Ct. 2004) aff'd 11 Misc. 3d 19 (N.Y. App. Term. 2005).

231   *Brodsky v. Match.com*, S.D.N.Y. 1:09-cv-05328.

232   2008-07211 [N.Y. 2d Dept 2-9-2010].

233   575 F.3d 981, 988 (9th Cir. 2009).

234   See question 9.7 (What should I include in the terms of use?).

235   "Creative Commons is a nonprofit corporation dedicated to making it easier for people to share and build upon the work of others, consistent with the rules of copyright. [They] provide free licenses and other legal tools to mark creative work with the freedom the creator wants it to carry, so others can share, remix, use commercially, or any combination thereof"; www.creativecommons.org.

CHAPTER 8

236   No. C 06-01802 MHP (N.D. Ca., Sept. 5, 2006).

237   *National Federation of the Blind et al., v. Target Corporation* (Case3:06-cv-01802-MHP Document214 Filed 08/03/09), United States District Court, Northern District of California.

238   At the time of the settlement, Target did not know it would also be paying National Federation's attorney fees.

239   www.ada.gov/anprm2010/web%20anprm_2010.htm

240   2003 WL 21406289 (C.D. Cal. Mar. 7, 2003).

241   2006 WL 361983 (N.D. Tex. Dec. 12, 2006).

242   456 US 844 (1982).

243   600 F. 3d 93 (C.A., 2nd 2010).

244   2010 WL 4455830 (S.D.N.Y. Nov. 4, 2010).

245   135 F. Supp. 2d 409 (S.D.N.Y. 2001).

246   658 F.3d 936 (9th Cir. 2011).

247   See http://www.census.gov/prod/2012pubs/p70-131.pdf

248   See the US Department of Justice ADA homepage at www.usdoj.gov/crt/ada/adahom1.htm

249   Opinion letter dated September 9, 1996, by the US Department of Justice.

250   For example, the Access Board (Architectural and Transportation Barriers Compliance Board) is the federal agency responsible for writing guidelines for (1) Section 508 of the Rehabilitation Act, (2) the ADA, (3) the Telecommunications Act of 1996, and (4) the Architec-

tural Barriers Act. Although they are still promulgating rules, it seems clear that electronic communications and website are to be covered by these guidelines; www.access-board.gov/508.htm.

251　No. C 06-01802 MHP (N.D. Ca., Sept. 5, 2006).

252　www.justice.gov/opa/pr/2010/July/10-crt-850.html

253　413 US 15 (1973).

254　*Miller v. California,* 413 US 15, at 25.

255　The Electronic Signatures in Global and National Commerce Act (ESIGN Act of 2000), 15 U.S.C. 96, is a federal law designed to address some differences in state law by providing that a contract or signature "may not be denied legal effect, validity, or enforceability solely because it is in electronic form." Thus, electronic signatures and records are just as good as their paper equivalents. Please note that certain types of contracts are excluded.

256　A fantastic source for federal and state laws regarding the sale of goods and services can be found at: http://business.ftc.gov/documents/bus01-businesspersons-guide-federal-warranty-law.

257　See FTC's Rule on Disclosure of Written Consumer Product Warranty Terms and Conditions at 16 C.F.R. Part 701.

258　See Section 102 of the Magnuson-Moss Act at 15 U.S.C. § 2301 et seq.

259　This is called an indemnification. Any written agreement in which you agree to sell on someone else's behalf should include this indemnification language. It will permit you to seek reimbursement from the person whose goods you are selling for and damages you are required to pay to a third party as a result of an injury, physical or monetary, with respect to the product. It may also require that person or entity to pay your attorney fees.

260　Steve Womack, "With Online Sales Tax, States Can Collect Revenue They Are Owed," *US News and World Report*, December 10, 2012, at www.usnews.com/opinion/articles/2012/12/10/with-online-sales-tax-states-can-collect-revenue-they-are-owed

261　"I think the Supreme Court got it right in 1992," Wood says. "I have no business collecting sales tax in Vermont, and I don't think the buyer there is going to understand why they have to pay it." She rejects the idea that the current system favors online retailers, noting that many physical stores also do Web sales and that shipping charges level the playing field substantially. She estimates it would take her six weeks a year to comply with sales tax procedures in the 45 sales tax-collecting states, which have close to 10,000 local jurisdictions that may charge different rates." This quote is from a former attorney, now seller on eBay. Karen E. Klein, "It's Retailer vs. Retailer in Internet Sales Tax Push," *Bloomberg Businessweek*, January 10, 2013, at www.businessweek.com/articles/2013-01-10/its-retailer-vs-dot-retailer-in-internet-sales-tax-push. On the other end of the spectrum are the states that wish to tap into the enormous potential for revenues without regard to the burden it would place on small Internet businesses.

262 481 F. Supp. 2d 575 (E.D. La. 2007).

263 John Blackstone, "Calif. law ends tax-free shopping for Amazon.com, other online retailers," *CBS This Morning*, September 14, 2012, at www.cbsnews.com/8301-505268_162-57512862/calif-law-ends-tax-free-shopping-for-amazon.com-other-online-retailers/

264 See www.ftc.gov

265 GLBA, 16 CFR 314.4(a)-(c).

266 www.leginfo.ca.gov/cgi-bin/displaycode?section=bpc&group=22001-23000&file=22575-22579

267 www.privacy.ca.gov/privacy_laws

268 See www.ncsl.org/default.aspx?tabid=13463 for information on other state privacy regulations.

269 Compgeeks.com's parent company is the Genica Corporation, which was also named in the enforcement action.

270 See www.ftc.gov/opa/2009/02/compgeeks.shtm

271 Much like the GLBA does.

272 *In The Matter of The TJX Companies, Inc.* FTC File No. 072-3055.

273 www.ftc.gov/opa/2008/03/datasec.shtm

274 www.ftc.gov/opa/2008/03/datasec.shtm

275 www.ftc.gov/os/caselist/0723055/080801tjxdo.pdf

276 15 U.S.C. Sections 7701-7713.

277 State laws regarding spam can be found at www.ncsl.org/issues-research/telecom/state-spam-laws.aspx.

278 www.leginfo.ca.gov/cgi-bin/displaycode?section=bpc&group=17001-18000&file=17529-17529.9

279 http://delcode.delaware.gov/title11/c005/sc03/index.shtml#937

280 See *United States v. Goodin*, Case No. 06-110 (C.D. Cal. 2007), and *Jaynes v. Commonwealth*, 48 Va. App. 673 (2006).

CHAPTER 9

281   To read what the FCC tells you to do if you are receiving unwanted commercial emails and texts, go to www.fcc.gov/guides/spam-unwanted-text-messages-and-email.

282   483 F. Supp. 2d 1058 - Dist. Court, D. Oregon 2007.

283   Geoffrey A. Fowler, "Facebook Sells More Access to Members," *Wall Street Journal*, October 1, 2012, at http://online.wsj.com/article/SB10000872396390443862604578029450918199258.html

284   Currently, California is the only state that requires websites to have a privacy policy.

285   Such technology includes firewalls, virus detection software, and encryption.

286   See www.ncsl.org/default.aspx?tabid=13463 for information on state privacy regulations.

287   The Children's Online Privacy Protection Act (COPPA), 15 U.S.C. 6501 et seq., became effective in 2000. The amendments became effective July 2013. When a website is directed towards children under the age of thirteen or knowingly has users under the age of thirteen, it must obtain verifiable consent from the parents prior to collecting data about the children. A "conspicuously posted" privacy policy is required that details the information collected and how it is used and shared. It also requires the website to take security measures to keep such information private. The COPPA rules can be found at 16 CFR Part 312.

288   *United States v. Iconix Brand Group*, FTC File No. 0923032.

289   The Children's Online Privacy Protection Act, effective April 21, 2000, applies to the online collection of personal information from children under thirteen. The new rules spell out what a website operator must include in a privacy policy, when and how to seek verifiable consent from a parent, and what responsibilities an operator has to protect children's privacy and safety online. The following is taken from the FTC website:

The Federal Trade Commission staff prepared this guide to help you comply with the new requirements for protecting children's privacy online and understand the FTC's enforcement authority.

WHO MUST COMPLY

If you operate a commercial Web site or an online service directed to children under 13 that collects personal information from children or if you operate a general audience Web site and have actual knowledge that you are collecting personal information from children, you must comply with the Children's Online Privacy Protection Act.

- To determine whether a Web site is directed to children, the FTC considers several factors, including the subject matter; visual or audio content; the age of models on the site; language; whether advertising on the Web site is directed to children; information regarding the age of the actual or intended audience; and whether a site uses animated characters or other child-oriented features.
- To determine whether an entity is an 'operator' with respect to information collected at a site, the FTC will consider who owns and controls the information; who pays for the collection and maintenance of the information; what the preexisting contractual relationships are in connection with the information; and what role the Web site plays in collecting or maintaining the information.

PERSONAL INFORMATION

The Children's Online Privacy Protection Act and Rule apply to individually identifiable information about a child that is collected online, such as full name, home address, email address, telephone number or any other information that would allow someone to identify or contact the child. The Act and Rule also cover other types of information—for example, hobbies, interests and information collected through cookies or other types of tracking mechanisms—when they are tied to individually identifiable information.

Basic Provisions

Privacy Notice

Placement

An operator must post a link to a notice of its information practices on the homepage of its Web site or online service and at each area where it collects personal information from children. An operator of a general audience site with a separate children's area must post a link to its notice on the homepage of the children's area.

The link to the privacy notice must be clear and prominent. Operators may want to use a larger font size or a different color type on a contrasting background to make it stand out. A link in small print at the bottom of the page—or a link that is indistinguishable from other links on your site—is not considered clear and prominent.

Content

- The notice must be clearly written and understandable; it should not include any unrelated or confusing materials. It must state the following information:
- The name and contact information (address, telephone number and email address) of all operators collecting or maintaining children's personal information through the Web site or online service. If more than one operator is collecting information at the site, the site may select and provide contact information for only one operator who will respond to all inquiries from parents about the site's privacy policies. Still, the names of all the operators must be listed in the notice.
- The kinds of personal information collected from children (for example, name, address, email address, hobbies, etc.) and how the information is collected—directly from the child or passively, say, through cookies.
- How the operator uses the personal information. For example, is it for marketing back to the child? Notifying contest winners? Allowing the child to make the information publicly available through a chat room?
- Whether the operator discloses information collected from children to third parties. If so, the operator also must disclose the kinds of businesses in which the third parties are engaged; the general purposes for which the information is used; and whether the third parties have agreed to maintain the confidentiality and security of the information.
- That the parent has the option to agree to the collection and use of the child's information without consenting to the disclosure of the information to third parties.
- That the operator may not require a child to disclose more information than is reasonably necessary to participate in an activity as a condition of participation.

- That the parent can review the child's personal information, ask to have it deleted and refuse to allow any further collection or use of the child's information. The notice also must state the procedures for the parent to follow.

DIRECT NOTICE TO PARENTS

Content

The notice to parents must contain the same information included on the notice on the Web site. In addition, an operator must notify a parent that it wishes to collect personal information from the child; that the parent's consent is required for the collection, use and disclosure of the information; and how the parent can provide consent. The notice to parents must be written clearly and understandably, and must not contain any unrelated or confusing information. An operator may use any one of a number of methods to notify a parent, including sending an email message to the parent or a notice by postal mail.

Verifiable Parental Consent

Before collecting, using or disclosing personal information from a child, an operator must obtain verifiable parental consent from the child's parent. This means an operator must make reasonable efforts (taking into consideration available technology) to ensure that before personal information is collected from a child, a parent of the child receives notice of the operator's information practices and consents to those practices.

Until April 2002, the FTC will use a sliding scale approach to parental consent in which the required method of consent will vary based on how the operator uses the child's personal information. That is, if the operator uses the information for internal purposes, a less rigorous method of consent is required. If the operator discloses the information to others, the situation presents greater dangers to children, and a more reliable method of consent is required. The sliding scale approach will sunset in April 2002 subject to a Commission review planned for October 2001.

For the entire text of the article, see http://business.ftc.gov/documents/bus84-childrens-online-privacy-protection-rule-six-step-compliance-plan-your-business

290 See 17 USC 512

291 Although there are not many cases involving this particular issue in the United States, one that comes to mind involves AOL's attempt to enforce a venue clause in its online terms of service. The online AOL contract indicated that subscribers agreed to bring suit against AOL only in AOL's home jurisdiction. While some courts enforced the clause, others have said it is not fair to force AOL users to sue AOL outside of their own state.

In an earlier case in which the FTC got involved, Spiegel, a Chicago-based mail order company, indicated in its terms of use that it could sue on delinquent accounts in Illinois courts, under Illinois' long-arm statute. This would allow Spiegel to easily obtain judgments against those out-of-state defendants who did not show up. When an out-of-state defendant did hire a lawyer to appear in Illinois and ask for a change of venue to his or her home state, Spiegel would dismiss the lawsuit.

The FTC filed a complaint against Spiegel claiming that its terms requiring out-of-state defendants to appear in Illinois courts were an "unfair trade practice" because of the burden put on such out-of-state defendants. The 7th Circuit held that the US Supreme Court "left no doubt that the FTC ha[s] the authority to prohibit conduct that, although legally proper, [i]s unfair to the public." Although this did not involve online terms of use, it is clear that the FTC can bring action to stop activities that are deemed to be deceptive or unfair.

What this means for you is that the FTC will be looking for unfair and deceptive trade practices. If your terms of use contain unfair terms or your website contains inaccurate or misleading information, the FTC could bring an action against you. However, other courts have permitted choice of law and choice of forum clauses when the users have affirmatively consented to the terms of use with these provisions clearly stated.

292 http://digitalcommons.law.scu.edu/cgi/viewcontent.cgi?article=1152 &context=historical

293 http://scholar.google.com/scholar_case?case=463283202431233064 1&hl=en&as_sdt=2&as_vis=1&oi=scholarr

294 See *Asmus v. Pacific Bell*, 23 Cal.4th 1, 15-16 (2000), and *Powell v. Central California Federal Savings and Loan Ass'n.*, 59 Cal.App. 3d 540 (1976).

295 218 F.Supp.2d 1165 (N.D. Cal. 2002).

296 In *Guadagno v. E-Trade Bank*, 592 F.Supp.2d 1263 (C.D. Cal. 2008), the court held that when a user is given the ability to opt out of a new term, the contract will not be deemed procedurally unconscionable.

297 [2009] EWCA Civ 717 Case No: B2/2009/0162.

298 Case Nos. 5:09-cv-03043-JF, 5:09-cv-03519-JF, 5:09-cv--03430-JF, Slip op. (N.D. Cal. Apr. 22, 2010).

299 It seems that the courts in the United States will require users to consent to your terms before they will find them binding. This is different in Europe, although the *Patchett v. SPATA* case indicates that a disclaimer may be valid if prominently displayed. In *Patchett*, the court found that a disclaimer placed on an "About Us" page of a website was sufficient notice to the users. In this case, the users were advised to request an information pack before entering into a contract with any company listed on the site, which was found to be reasonable.

CHAPTER 10

300 No. 08-1393, 2010 US App. LEXIS 1931 (10th Cir. Jan. 28, 2010).

301 See question 10.9 (Do I have to get a license to operate an in-home Internet business?).

302 Retrieved from www.sba.gov/smallbusinessplanner/start/choosea-structure/. Please also check with the irs.gov website or an accountant for any forms not listed here.

303 Note that there are other legal structures that fall under the heading of partnerships: a limited partnership, a limited liability partner-ship, and a limited liability limited partnership. These forms of ownership may be recommended to you by your accountant. "Limited" means that some of the partners have limited liability (to the extent of their initial investment) and limited input regarding management decisions, which generally encourages investing in short-term projects or capital assets. A limited partnership requires at least one general partner and a written agreement, and is more complex and formal than a general partnership. A joint venture is similar to a general partnership but is formed for a limited time or project. Please consult both an accountant and an attorney for more information.

304 Retrieved from www.sba.gov/smallbusinessplanner/start/choosea-structure/. Please also check with the irs.gov website or an accountant for any forms not listed here.

305 There are certain professions that may incorporate as a professional corporation. If you are an accountant, attorney, doctor, or dentist, you may wish to look into this legal structure.

306 Most small businesses file the charter in the state in which they are located, but certain advantages may be gained by filing elsewhere. Your accountant or attorney may discuss your options with you.

307 Note that most boards select the officers who actually manage the day-to-day operations of the business. Many times, the shareholder, board, and officers are the same people in small corporations.

308 They can become liable under certain circumstances, such as failing to meet the legal requirements of maintaining the corporation's legal status, or for certain types of torts.

309 In order to qualify for a subchapter S status, see the next question.

310 Retrieved from www.sba.gov/smallbusinessplanner/start/choosea-structure/. Please also check with the irs.gov website or an accountant for any forms not listed here.

311 This double-taxation can be avoided if the corporation elects a subchapter S status if certain requirements are met. This allows a corporation to pass through its taxes to the shareholder.

312 Retrieved from www.sba.gov/smallbusinessplanner/start/choosea-structure/. Please also check with the irs.gov website or an accountant for any forms not listed here.

313 Note that not every state permits this type of organization and that the rules are different in each state.

314 An LLC may, however, choose to be taxed like a corporation.

315 Retrieved from www.sba.gov/smallbusinessplanner/start/choosea-structure/. Please also check with the irs.gov website or an accountant for any forms not listed here.

316 Please refer to the question 10.1 (If I have an Internet business, do I need to incorporate?).

317 Some states require licenses based on professions (e.g., contractors and cosmetologists) or type of goods sold (e.g., liquor and firearms).

318 This is usually the Secretary of State's office.

319 This is usually required in states with a state income tax.

320   See http://www.sba.gov/content/employment-and-labor-law for a list of the many laws regarding employment issues.

321   See www.irs.gov/pub/irs-pdf/p1779.pdf, which is an IRS publication that explains the difference between and independent contractor and an employee.

322   See http://www.sba.gov/content/hire-your-first-employee for complete details on these steps.

323   See http://www.sba.gov/content/learn-about-your-state-and-local-tax-obligations for links to all of the states.

324   See http://www.nfib.com/legal-center/compliance-resource-center/compliance-resource-item/cmsid/57181 for each state's workers compensation laws.

325   See http://www.sba.gov/content/learn-about-your-state-and-local-tax-obligations for links to each state's tax departments.

326   See http://www.sba.gov/content/learn-about-your-state-and-local-tax-obligations for links to these state's tax departments.

327   See http://www.sba.gov/content/workplace-posters for more information.

328   47 USC Sec. 230(c)(2).

329   17 USC Sec. 512.

330   Art Brodsky, "PIPA And SOPA Were Stopped, but the Web Hasn't Won," *The Huffington Post*, January 25, 2012, at www.huffingtonpost.com/art-brodsky/pipa-and-sopa-were-stoppe_b_1230818.html This article details some of the other proposed legislation that was defeated in recent years that you may have forgotten.

331   Please note that I am not hoping that these areas are legislated; I am only noting that there is a great deal of disparity on how these issues are being handled.

INDEX

191

ABOUT THE AUTHOR

Kimberly A. Houser is a business consultant, attorney, professor, and writer, who has been counseling clients and lecturing on Internet law and e-commerce issues for over a decade. She graduated from the University of Texas in 1984 with a Bachelor of Business Administration and earned her law degree from the University of Illinois in 1987. Kimberly is a Clinical Associate Professor of Business Law for Washington State University, which allows her to stay current with the ever-changing legal issues that arise in the domain of information technology. She is well known for being able to break down complicated legal issues into manageable pieces.

Her primary research area involves exploring the paradox of applying current laws to emerging technologies. Kimberly is also the author of *Survey of American Law*, an introductory law textbook for undergraduate students and has been published in the Illinois Bar Journal and the International Journal of Business and Public Administration. She is the recipient of a Rickert Award in Excellence in Clinical Legal Education and an Am Jur in Trial Advocacy. She is also a member of the Legal Writing Institute, the Academy of Legal Studies in Business, and the Cyber Law and Data Privacy Section of the Chicago Bar Association.

The inception of this book began years ago, when Kimberly was searching for a legal guide she could recommend to her business clients who were beginning to set up websites and discovered that there were not any such books out there. She started putting together a notebook with a collection of articles, cases, and blog posts covering the legal issues involved in taking a business online. When she learned that more and more of her clients were posting content on social media and other websites, she added that information as well. She was shocked to discover clients posting false reviews of their services, copying from other websites without authorization, and collecting personal information from their customers without informing them of the collection activities. She realized at this point that the legal issues were much larger than her clients understood. Because of the recent explosion in social media usage, she turned her notebook into manuscript in order to share the information she collected.

Kimberly is passionate about educating and helping people. She will often talk with her clients for hours, discussing their problems and concerns (even when their "official" time is up). She wrote the *Legal Guide to Social Media* because there are no other books like it. She wants not only her clients, but also all users of social media to become aware of the risks in posting content. Because of the increasing numbers and sizes of judgments in this area of law, she feels strongly about educating the public and making these simple protection strategies available to everyone. Kimberly lives in Pullman, Washington. She enjoys Words with Friends, many outdoor activities, and discussing libertarian ideals.

Books from Allworth Press

Allworth Press is an imprint of Skyhorse Publishing, Inc. Selected titles are listed below.

Starting Your Career as a Social Media Manager
By Mark Story (6 x 9, 264 pages, paperback, $19.95)

Branding for Bloggers
By Zack Heller (5 ½ x 8 ½, 112 pages, paperback, $16.95)

Starting Your Career as a Professional Blogger
By Jacqueline Bodnar (6 x 9, 192 pages, paperback, $19.95)

The Pocket Legal Companion to Copyright
By Lee Wilson (5 x 7 ½, 336 pages, paperback, $16.95)

The Pocket Legal Companion to Trademark
By Lee Wilson (5 x 7 ½, 320 pages, paperback, $16.95)

The Pocket Small Business Owner's Guide to Building Your Business
By Kevin Devine (5 ¼ x 8 ¼, 256 pages, paperback, $14.95)

The Pocket Small Business Owner's Guide to Starting Your Business on a Shoestring
By Carol Tice (5 ¼ x 8 ¼, 244 pages, paperback, $14.95)

The Art of Digital Branding, Revised Edition
By Ian Cocoran (6 x 9, 272 pages, paperback, $19.95)

Brand Thinking and Other Noble Pursuits
By Debbie Millman (6 x 9, 336 pages, hardcover, $29.95)

Emotional Branding
By Marc Gobé (6 x 9, 352 pages, paperback, $19.95)

Business and Legal Forms for Authors and Self-Publishers
By Tad Crawford (8 ½ x 11, 192, paperback, $22.95)

The Business of Writing
Edited by Jennifer Lyons (6 x 9, 304 pages, paperback, $19.95)

The Writer's Legal Guide, Fourth Edition
By Kay Murray and Tad Crawford (6 x 9, 352 pages, paperback, $19.95)

Fine Art Publicity
By Susan Abbott (6 x 9, 192 pages, paperback, $19.95)

Legal Guide for the Visual Artist, Fifth Edition
By Tad Crawford (8 ½ x 11, 304 pages, paperback, $29.95)

Starting Your Career as a Freelance Web Designer
By Neil Tortorella (6 x 9, 256 pages, paperback, $19.95)

To see our complete catalog or to order online, please visit *www.allworth.com*.